BOBBY CREMINS'
Ultimate Offense

Winning Basketball Strategies and Plays from an NCAA Coach's Personal Playbook

---

BOBBY CREMINS

New York   Chicago   San Francisco   Lisbon   London   Madrid   Mexico City
Milan   New Delhi   San Juan   Seoul   Singapore   Sydney   Toronto

*The **McGraw·Hill** Companies*

Library of Congress Cataloging-in-Publication Data

Cremins, Bobby, 1947–
     Bobby Cremins' ultimate offense : winning basketball strategies and plays from an
NCAA coach's personal playbook / Bobby Cremins.
        p.   cm.
     Includes index.
     ISBN-13: 978-0-07-147917-2 (alk. paper)
     ISBN-10:   0-07-147917-1 (alk. paper)
     1. Basketball—Offense.   I. Title.   II. Title: Bobby Cremins' ultimate offense.
III. Title: Ultimate offense.

   GV889.C74   2009
   796.323'2—dc22   2008018188

1 2 3 4 5 6 7 8 9 10 11 12 13 14 15 16 17 18 19 20   DOC/DOC   0 9 8

ISBN 978-0-07-147917-2
MHID   0-07-147917-1

McGraw-Hill books are available at special quantity discounts to use as premiums and
sales promotions or for use in corporate training programs. To contact a representative,
please visit the Contact Us pages at www.mhprofessional.com.

This book is printed on acid-free paper.

Contents

Preface

The purpose of *Ultimate Offense* is to help you develop a free-flowing offense for your team—an offense where players don't have to think too much but rather react and play naturally, freely, and, of course, as a team. An offense can't be predictable, and players must have different options that they can execute on their own. *Ultimate Offense* lays out the type of mentality your team needs to fall in love with the running game. It shows you how to go from the primary to the all-important secondary break. The secondary break will have lots of options, and this book challenges and helps you to select the right ones for your team. Your secondary break should flow into your offense and, when you need to, run some half-court sets versus both man and zone defenses. There will be some great special plays, whether it be a lob or backdoor to use at the right time.

Many coaches today love to press and disrupt their opponents' offense. *Ultimate Offense* shows you how to attack pressure and keep the offensive flow going. Again, you will be challenged to know your personnel ex-

tremely well and choose which players should have what responsibilities. A simple decision, such as who will inbound the ball for you, can make or break your offense. Putting the right personnel in the right spots will be decided by experimenting in practice and getting to know your players' strengths and weaknesses. Moving one player to the correct position can dramatically improve your offense.

Chapter 5, "Special Situations," shows you the importance of late-game situations and how paramount it is to work on them. Your biggest challenge will be to find the time to do special situations in your practices. The quicker you get your offense down, the more time you can have to work on special situations. Once you start doing these situations, you'll quickly see their importance to a successful season.

I've been very fortunate to coach some great point guards, starting with Mark Price. I wanted to share why and how they were recruited and what I learned from them. Hopefully, their stories will interest you and show you the importance of the point guard position. I feel this book will get you thinking, give you some new ideas, get you to study your personnel, and help you to form your own free-flowing offense.

Writing this book has made me a better coach, and I hope that reading *Ultimate Offense* will do the same for you.

Introduction:
Why Up-Tempo Basketball?
(and Maybe Why Not)

Teaching the fast break was always step one of building our offense. Personally, I love fast break basketball and seeing a well executed 3 on 2, 2 on 1, or swinging the ball around for a wide open 3 is still one of the most exciting plays in the game today.

In my 25 plus years as a head coach the most dramatic rule change was the 3 point line. The addition of the 3 point line made the fast break even more important. Defensive transition was always taught to run to the lane and defend inside to outside. Defend like that today and you can really get burned from 3 point land. Now you have to find those shooters outside the line. Up-tempo basketball gets you many great looks from outside the arc.

When you play up-tempo basketball you put tremendous pressure on the defense. You never allow them time to set their defense and this keeps them off balanced. Many coaches play up-tempo simply to wear their opponents down. It allows them to play more players and spread that playing time around. These coaches also have excellent strength and conditioning programs to coincide with their up-tempo philosophy.

The most incredible fast break team I ever watched was Paul Westhead's Loyola of Marymount team. Their average offensive possession was 6 seconds. That's right—6 seconds. Meeting with Paul one time I decided to switch gears and talk some half court sets. Paul looked at me and said, "Bobby, we don't run any half court offense—just fast break."

In the 1989–90 season they averaged 122.4 points per game and finished 26–6. Our paths came very close to passing that year. I'll never forget Bo Kimble shooting a left-handed free throw to honor his teammate Hank Gathers who tragically collapsed and died in their conference tournament. Without Hank they upset New Mexico State in the first round of the NCAAs, and beat Michigan 149–115 where their guard Jeff Fryer made eleven 3s. Alabama decided not to run with them in their next game but Loyola prevailed 62–60. They lost in the Elite Eight to UNLV 131–101. We, Georgia Tech, with our Lethal Weapon 3 of Kenny

Anderson, Dennis Scott, and Brian Oliver, lost to UNLV 91–80 in the Final Four semi-final game in Denver. Of course Jerry Tarkanian's running rebels went on to beat Duke the next game for the national championship.

I often wonder what our game plan would have been if Loyola had beaten UNLV. Like Jerry did, I feel certain we would have kept our up-tempo philosophy. I like telling Loyola's story not only because of the emotion of Bo and Hank but here a small Catholic school with its up-tempo philosophy almost made it to the Final Four. The year before, they scored 181 points in one game. Now that's taking fast break basketball to a whole new level.

CONCERNS OF UP-TEMPO BASKETBALL

Two major concerns you must keep an eye on in using up-tempo basketball are taking quick shots and shooting too many 3s.

Taking Quick Shots

Shot selection is a real offensive key for many coaches. Very rarely can you win taking poor shots. I've been blessed with some great shooters, Dennis Scott among them. Dennis had very long range and could fire from any distance, and he obviously loved the 3 point shot. His most made was 11 against Houston, and he averaged about 15 attempts per game. I sometimes had to pull Dennis in and go over shot

selection. Dennis had a great attitude because the last thing I wanted to do was tell him to stop shooting. He knew exactly where the 3 point line was and used it to his advantage at all times. His shot could bring the house down, and I have never seen such deflated defensive faces after Dennis would hit one of his bombs.

Another time we were playing a very good Kentucky team without Dennis. We took quick shots, got down a lot early, and never recovered. It was one of my worst coaching days. When I see that happening today, I immediately call timeout and tell our team no 3s unless it comes from inside outside. In other words, get the ball low for a high percentage shot or kick it out for a wide open 3.

One of my best coaching buddies, Les Robinson, was coaching Citadel against North Carolina, and at the time they were playing with players like James Worthy and company. Les told his team they were only taking two shots tonight —lay-ups and free throws. Citadel led 17–14 at the half. With 2 minutes to go, North Carolina was up 2 and Coach Dean Smith ordered his famous 4 corners. North Carolina hung on for the win but it was one of Les's finest coaching moments. Had Les run with North Carolina, Citadel could have lost by 50.

Two other coaches I have coached against who can control tempos are Dick Tarrant of Richmond and John Kresse of College of Charleston where I now coach. Dick and John ran great half court sets and wanted games in the 60s and low 70s. They both have upsets over highly ranked team including yours truly. In the ACC Dave Odum, then at Wake

Forest, now at South Carolina, was also excellent at controlling tempo.

Shooting Too Many 3s

Great football teams have offensive balance in passing and running. I feel there must be that type of balance in post and perimeter scoring. Most scoring today comes from the perimeter and that's okay as long as there is some post presence or threat. I have watched teams live and die with the 3-ball. When it's on they usually win; however, when they're off it can get ugly.

3 point attempt stats are an indicator I watch for in determining whether or not my teams have had good offensive balance. I can see it on our game tapes, for instance, if we shot too many 3s and had no post presence. The next day's practice would be emphasizing post scoring. You can say, "No 3 point shooting until you score 10 points in the paint." This also makes your perimeter players drive and attack the rim.

I always have some offensive sets that end up with our posts with the ball. Should I see too many 3s I'll immediately call these sets so we can get the ball inside. When I call these sets our team knows we're trying to go inside, and again it can settle down too much perimeter shooting. I'll show you some of these post sets in Chapter 3. This challenge of maintaining offensive balance is a major key to success.

BEING YOURSELF

I learned early in my career from many great coaches to always be yourself and do what you strongly believe in. If you need to control tempo to win and that is what you believe in, then do just that. The number one responsibility of a coach is to give his team a chance to win. Remember, you're running up-tempo basketball for specific reasons that will give your team offensive balance, chemistry, excitement, and success.

Terms Used in This Book

attack When the offense is going forward instead of sideways, north to south, not east to west

back-screen A screen is set from the back

ball side elbow The ball side elbow is the upper foul line corner on the side where the ball is

box sets Like corners of a box

box-and-one defense 1 defender plays man, the other 4 play a zone

bread-and-butter plays Your key man-to-man or zone plays

close the deal Maintaining your lead for the victory

corner runner Players running baseline to baseline

cut through Running through the middle of the court

ducks in The post on the weak side block steps into the lane, looking for a pass

fast-break look 5 players running to their spots on a made basket

flashing high Post coming high to receive the pass

freelancing Playing off instincts, not set play

go-to plays Getting the ball in your best player's hands

high flare screen The post comes high to screen the point or wing

high-low post attack High post passes to the low post

high-percentage shot A shot that has a very good chance of being made

inbounded The pass is made from out of bounds into the court

live and dead-ball looks Live looks is when the clock is running; dead-ball looks is when the clock is stopped

lob play high pass outside the rim where the receiver catches the ball and dunks it or shoots it in the air

long corner This is the corner furthest away from the ball being inbounded

looks low A player looks to throw a pass to the low post

perimeter players Players who are outside the arc

pops out Sets a screen and steps out for the pass

post flash play Pass to the post in the middle

post trail The post player behind the point on the break

post-cross screen 2 posts screening low for each other

posts up Gets to block on ball side

pressure defense The defense picks up full court

rim lane Running directly to the opposite basket

rolls low The post sets a screen and goes from the high to low post

run-and-jump This is when you double team the ball

saddle-dribbles Dribbling sideways

scouting This is studying your opponents' tendencies and can help a coach learn a lot about a player or team

short corner The corner nearest the ball being in bounded

shortcut the play Defense anticipates the play and makes a steal

sideline long Inbounding the ball on the opponent's side of the court

skip-pass Passing to a player one or 2 men removed from you

slides up A player goes from the low post to the high post

spot up FInd an open area to receive the pass

stacks set 2 players on both blocks, one above the other

staggered screen 2 screens set one after the other, not side by side

step out Going from inbound to out of bounds

swings to The ball is passed from the side to the middle or vice versa

three-quarter-court diamond press A team puts on full court pressure in a diamond-shape (1 man in the front, 2 in the middle, and 1 in the rear)

weak side The side opposite the ball

"X" move 1 post going low, other post coming high

zone traps 2 defenders in a zone, trapping the ball

Key to Diagrams

Player

Opposing player

Player with ball at beginning of sequence

Player moving

Player dribbling

Player passing

Screen

Passing options

Dribbling option

Running options

Skip pass

Player movement
(black to gray, to
lighter gray as the
play progresses)

CHAPTER 1

Transition Basketball: Implementing the Fast Break

There are two types of fast break to teach: made and missed shots. We start with the made shot for teaching reasons, but obviously we prefer the missed-shot break. There are also two stages of the fast break: primary and secondary. Primary options come early in the break while secondary options take you into offensive sets.

LIVE MADE BASKET

Teaching made baskets first will provide your offensive foundation, which will then carry over to your missed-shot break.

To start with, you must identify your best option for inbounding the ball. Made baskets are usually inbounded by post players 4 or 5. If they're not good inbounders, it is vital for you to practice teaching them how to inbound, or modify your break and let the 3, 2, or even 1 take it out. This could slow down your break, but first and foremost is inbounding the ball properly.

On late-game dead-ball situations, we have our 2 or 3 take it out, which I will demonstrate

in Chapter 2 ("Attacking Pressure") and Chapter 5 ("Special Situations"). In all my years of coaching live made baskets, I have allowed our post guys (4 or 5) to take it out. If we played a constant pressing team like Gary Williams's University of Maryland team or Rick Pitino's University of Kentucky team (now University of Louisville), we went to our dead-ball look the entire game where 2 or 3 inbounded.

Some years our 5 man was not a good inbounder and then we specifically wanted our 4 man to inbound on made shots. When I was hired July 3, 2006, by the College of Charleston, I immediately asked Mark Byington, an assistant under the previous staff who I kept on, "Which post men could inbound the ball the best?" Mark's answer quickly made me realize that only our 4 man would inbound on made baskets, while our 5 man would run the middle lane.

Another very important point you need to be thinking about is, do you want your trail post to stop above the 3-point circle—either to catch and swing the ball, shoot the 3, or even put it on the floor—or do you want your trail post to screen away for the weak side wing?

1

Without a doubt, the best trail post player I ever coached against was Duke University's Shane Battier. He possessed all the key traits. A smart, excellent passer, he could shoot the 3 and put it on the floor. Shane was exceptionally difficult to guard in transition. He's been an undersized 4 man as a pro in the National Basketball Association (NBA), but these qualities have helped him become an excellent NBA player.

I always allowed our trail post to stop and catch, but looking back there were a couple of years I wish I had our trail post screen away, especially when our 5 man had trouble swinging the ball and was no threat to shoot the 3. In this case, I basically had our 5 man screen on the ball and roll to the basket.

I will show you both ways, but you should do what's best for your personnel and what you feel comfortable teaching. This is all part of the great challenge of coaching: what system do you want to teach, and can you make coaching adjustments? I've seen coaches who never change their system and others, when things were not going well, make adjustments, and turn their whole season around.

If you do not like your system and want an entire overhaul, it's better to make major changes in the off-season with your staff. However, never be afraid to tweak it a little if you're not satisfied with your team's performance.

Meeting with my new staff at the College of Charleston, we came up with a fast-break system that gave our trail post a couple of choices. He could (a) catch the ball or (b) screen on the ball. These choices led to different offensive schemes.

Two things you must constantly be looking at in your fast break are the outlet and running lanes. The outlet is between your inbounder and receiver (likely your point guard). This outlet has to be quick and sharp. A simple but effective drill involves two posts and one point (Diagram 1.1).

Outlet Drills

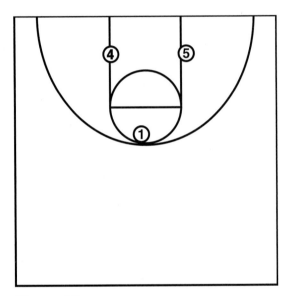

Diagram 1.1

- 4 grabs the made basket and quickly inbounds away from the backboard to 1, who is coming foul line extended to meet the pass and start the break.
- 5 is off and running the middle lane directly to the opposite rim (Diagram 1.2).

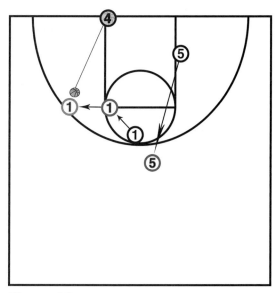

Diagram 1.2

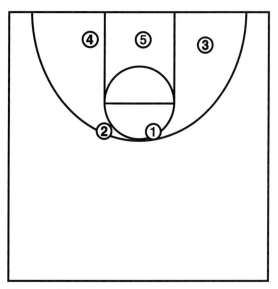

Diagram 1.4

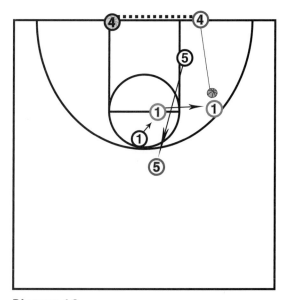

Diagram 1.3

In Diagram 1.3, starting from the same formation as the previous drill, you'll notice 1 going to the weak side. 1 has the freedom to do this, especially if he is being closely guarded.

- 1's job is to get open, get the ball, and get the break going.
- 4's job is to get the ball to 1.

Obviously, on made shots, your inbounder can run the baseline, but never on a violation.

- Three players—5, 2, and 3—will be running lanes all out. 2 and 3 must run wide and run to the opposite baseline deep in the corner. If either 2 or 3 cuts to the block and does not receive the pass, he must cut back out to his respective corner area, unless of course there is a shot attempt, whereas 2 and 3 are crashing the boards.
- 5 runs the middle to the opposite rim, where he posts up in the lane or the ball side block (Diagrams 1.4 and 1.5).

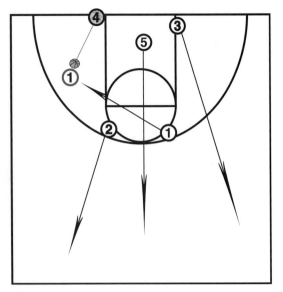

Diagram 1.5

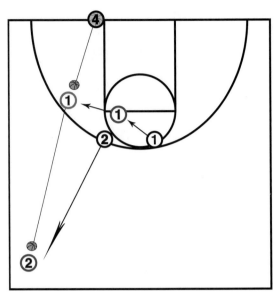

Diagram 1.6

Note: As previously mentioned, 5 takes the middle lane. 2, the better wing shooter, takes the ball side lane. 3, the better rebounding wing, takes the weak side lane. 2 and 3 will be interchangeable on our missed-shot break, but on a made shot they usually have assigned lanes. However, should you prefer, they can be interchangeable on made shots also.

From here we are able to teach our primary break options.

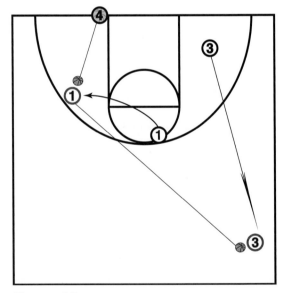

Diagram 1.7

Primary Break Options—
After 4-1 Outlet

1-2

1 makes a quick sideline pass to 2 for a layup or jump shot (Diagram 1.6).

1-3

1 makes a quick crosscourt pass to 3 for a layup or jump shot (see Diagram 1.7).

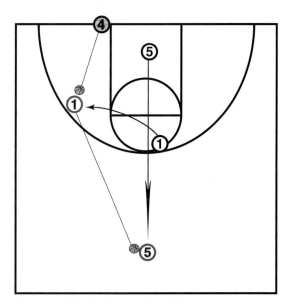

Diagram 1.8 1-5 Primary Break Option

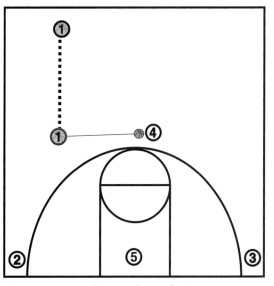

Diagram 1.9 1-4 Primary Break Option

1-5

1 makes a lead pass to 5 for a layup or a dunk (Diagram 1.8).

1-4

1 makes a swing-pass to 4 for a layup or jump shot (Diagram 1.9).

1

The point guard keeps his dribble alive and penetrates or pulls up for a jump shot (Diagram 1.10). A great primary break drill is to get everyone a layup—1-2, 1-3, 1-5, 1-4, and 1—within 30 seconds. It teaches quick outlets from 4 to 1 and fast running lanes from 2, 3, and 4.

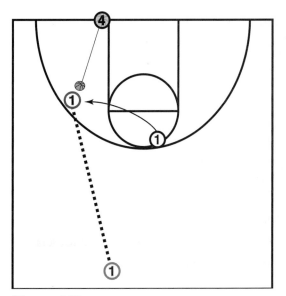

Diagram 1.10

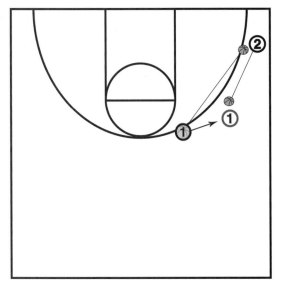

Diagram 1.11 1-2-1 Option

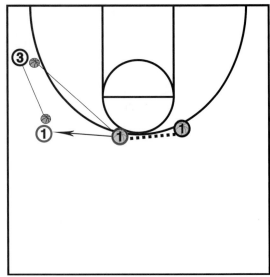

Diagram 1.12 1-3-1 Option

More Primary Break Options

1-2-1

1 passes ahead and follows the pass to get it back. It is important to let 1 know he can get the ball back after passing ahead and that, secondly, he must stay wide for spacing purposes (Diagram 1.11).

1-3-1

1 crosses over to 3's side, passes ahead, and follows the pass in order to get it back from 3. Again, 1 must stay wide (Diagram 1.12).

Note: After 1 receives the outlet pass, he can stay on the ball side or come to the middle as he sees fit. I prefer to allow him the freedom to do both and even cross over to the weak side if he wants. We run our break options exactly the same from either side.

I have been asked many times, "Should your point guard pass ahead or dribble up the court?" I do want our point guard to pass ahead when someone is wide open; otherwise, he can keep his dribble alive. This has to be a natural judgment by your point guard. Should he be missing wide-open lanes ahead, teach him to pass ahead or to "give it up" until you trust his judgment.

1-2-5, 1-3-5, 1-2-3, and 1-3-2 as Primary Break Options

The post player (non-inbounder) running the middle lane to the rim posts up on the ball side block. We want him with his hands up, body wide, and fighting for scoring position. We want him above the block so he does not make a move behind the backboard. This is a

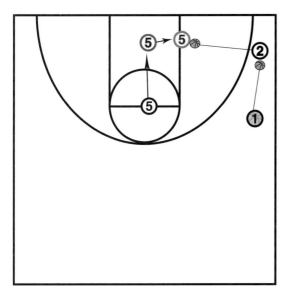

Diagram 1.13 1-2-5 Option

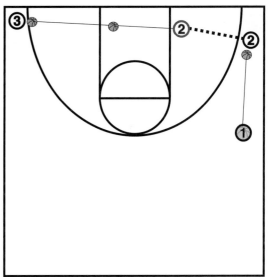

Diagram 1.15 1-2-3 Option

1-2-3

1 passes ahead to 2, who drives the baseline and skip-passes to 3 in the opposite deep corner (Diagram 1.15).

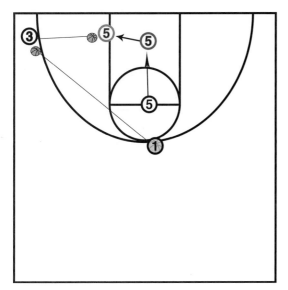

Diagram 1.14 1-3-5 option

very high percentage shot, and we work hard in our post shooting drills to teach moves like the power drop step, jump hook, and pivot crossover so we can score in this area (Diagrams 1.13 and 1.14).

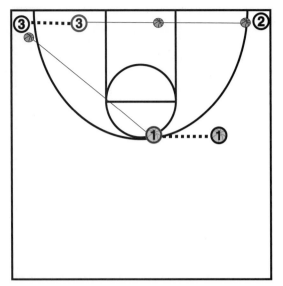

Diagram 1.16 1-3-2 Option

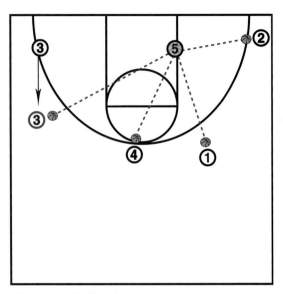

Diagram 1.17 Spot Up

1-3-2

1 passes to 3, who drives the baseline and skip-passes to 2 in the opposite deep corner (Diagram 1.16).

Low Post Motion

Whenever your post catches the ball, you must have passing outlets for him should the defense double-team or trap the post area. You can either spot up (diagram 1.17) or you can cut to the basket. The passer (2) can cut with 1 filling in for 2, 4 shifting toward 1, and 3 shifting toward 4 (Diagrams 1.18 and 1.19).

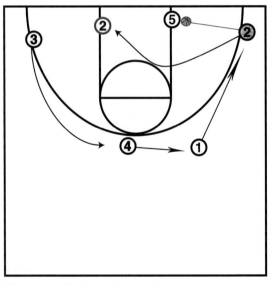

Diagram 1.18 Passer Basket Cutter

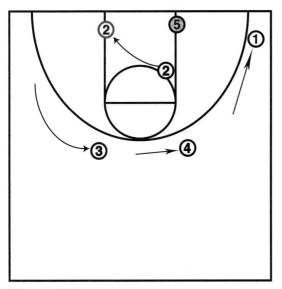

Diagram 1.19

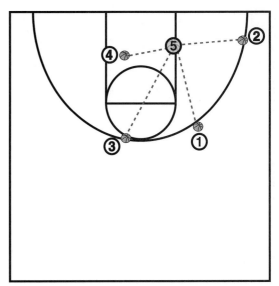

Diagram 1.21

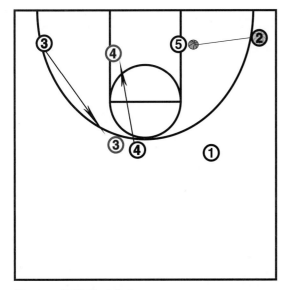

Diagram 1.20 Post Cut

passing options out of the double team. You must teach your post to think like a point guard when he's double-teamed and find the open man. Teach your post to face outward away from the baseline in order to find his open teammates.

Or 4 can cut with 3 filling in for 4 (Diagrams 1.20 and 1.21).

Most teams will double-team your post, so having cutters and positioning your weak side shooters gives your post plenty of excellent

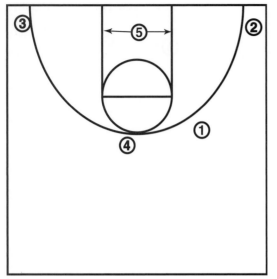

Diagram 1.22

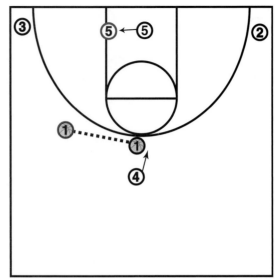

Diagram 1.24

We always run to 4-out, 1-in motion (Diagram 1.22).

The inbounder/trail post (4) stays opposite and above 1. If 1 crosses over, 4 crosses over to stay opposite (Diagrams 1.23 and 1.24).

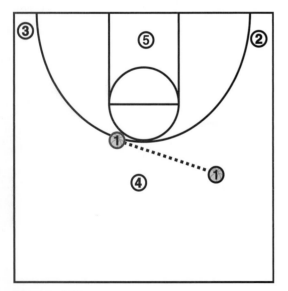

Diagram 1.23

Swing Pass This is the all-important pass that takes you from your primary break to the secondary and on into your motion offense.

You can swing it by, (a) 4 catching 1 pass (Diagram 1.25), (b) 4 screening away for weak side wing to catch pass from 1 (Diagram 1.26), (c) or 4 screening for 1 allowing 1 to swing it himself (Diagram 1.27).

Important Decision Again, just a reminder that you must decide whether or not you want your post man to stop at the top of the 3-point line above the line of the ball or whether you want your trail post to screen away or even just screen on the ball. Don't forget, should your post be able to catch, pass, and put it on the floor, then you're smart to stop him at the top of the 3-point line. If not, he can screen away for the weak side wing. It's your choice, but it goes a long

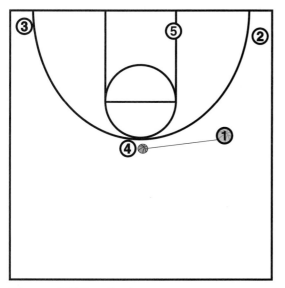

Diagram 1.25 Post Catch

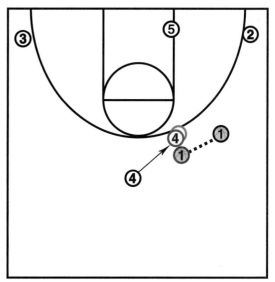

Diagram 1.27 Post Screen on Ball

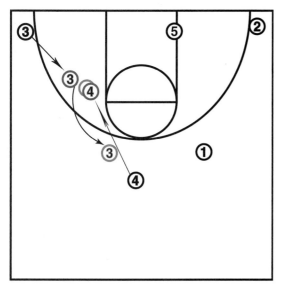

Diagram 1.26 Post Screen Away

away. Those teams had post players who struggled swinging the ball, shooting 3s, and putting it on the floor. When you have turnovers swinging the ball, look to take the pressure off your post and let him screen away for a better ball handler. I love the post trail screening on the ball. It's simple and effective.

way in determining the type of offense you will have.

I always stop our trail post at the top with an option to screen on the ball. Looking back, I did have teams that I wished I had screened

Guard Through

Before we get to the swing pass, we have another option for the point where he passes to the wing and cuts through to the weak side block (Diagram 1.28).

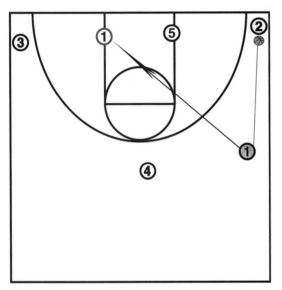

Diagram 1.28

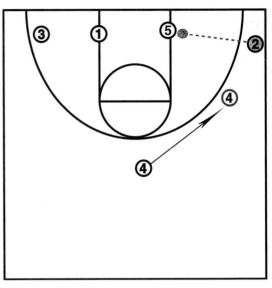

Diagram 1.29

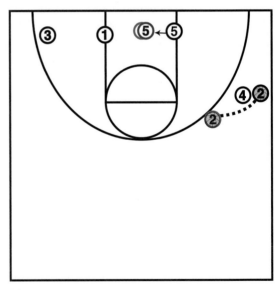

Diagram 1.30

- The trail post (4) reads this pass and immediately starts coming to set a high ball side screen for 2.
- 2's first option when he catches 1's pass is to look inside to 5. Then 2 starts looking for 4's screen (Diagram 1.29).
- Once 2 starts using 4's screen, 5 screens across for 1 (Diagram 1.30).

- After 4 screens for 2, 4 sets a second post screen for 1. 1 is now using a double post staggered screen (Diagram 1.31).
- 2 is looking to penetrate and make a play. He can look to score, pass inside to

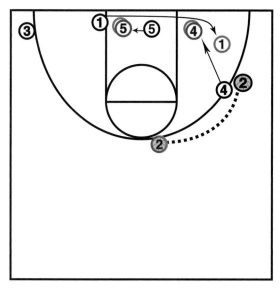

Diagram 1.31

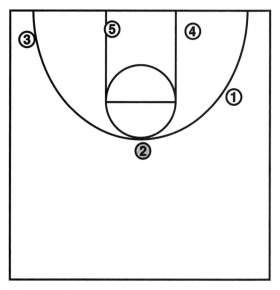

Diagram 1.33

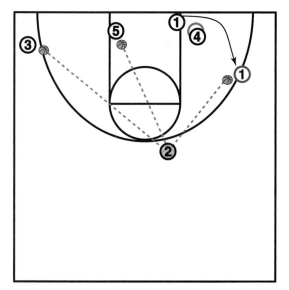

Diagram 1.32

• On 2's pass to 3 or back to 1, you're in 3-out, 2-in motion (Diagram 1.33).

a post, who is ducking in, or pass weak side to 3, and, of course, he is looking back to 1 coming off the post staggered screens (Diagram 1.32).

Swing Pass

- Your point now decides to pass to 4. On this pass, he cuts to the ball side block.
- 5 is searching the ball looking for a high/low pass from 4.
- When 4 catches the ball, he has lots of options. He can shoot, drive, pass to 5, swing to the weak side (3), or even swing back to the ball side wing (2) (Diagram 1.34).

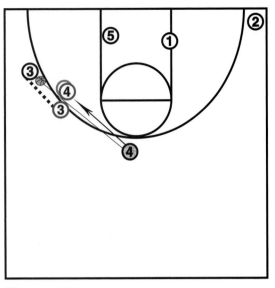

Diagram 1.35

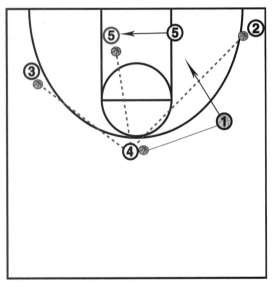

Diagram 1.34

- Should 4 swing to the weak side wing (3), 4 will follow his pass to set a high side screen for 3 (Diagram 1.35).

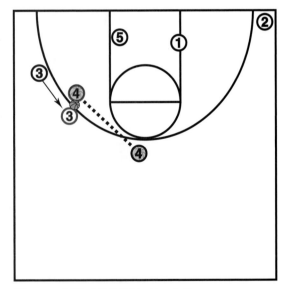

Diagram 1.36 4-3 Dribble Handoff

- Should 4 feel uncomfortable swinging the ball to 3, 4 can make a dribble handoff to 3 (Diagram 1.36).

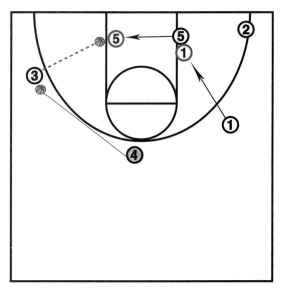

Diagram 1.37

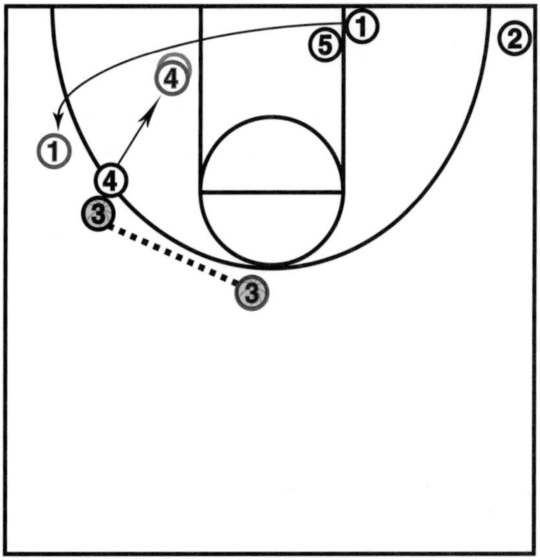

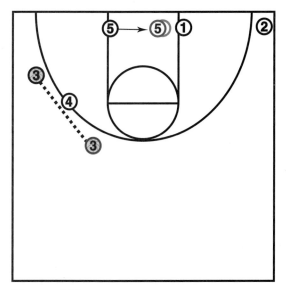

Diagram 1.38

Diagram 1.39

- After using 4's screen, 4 continues down to set a second post screen for 1 (Diagram 1.39).

- Should 4 pass to 3, 3's first option is to look low to 5 (Diagram 1.37).
- 3 then uses 4's high side screen.
- Once 3 uses 4's screen, 5 screens across for 1 (Diagram 1.38).

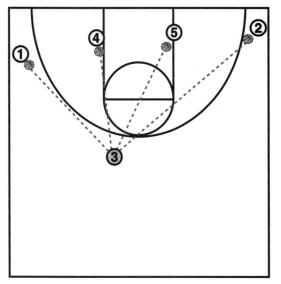

Diagram 1.40

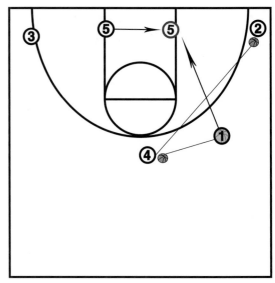

Diagram 1.41

- Like 2, in guard-through action, 3 can penetrate, pass low to the post, pass weak side to 2, and, of course, go back to 1 coming off the double post staggered screen. On any pass to the wing, you're in 3-out, 2-in motion (Diagram 1.40).

4 Back to 2 Ball Side Wing

- 4 passes back to the ball side wing (2) (Diagram 1.41). This is another excellent option for 4 and can be used as a set call or play.

- On this pass, 1 will now set a cross screen for 5 (Diagram 1.42).
- After passing to 2, 4 will down-screen the screener (1).

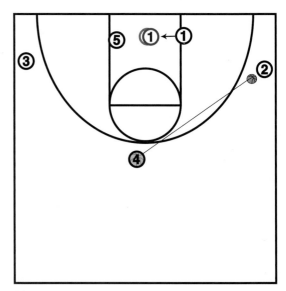

Diagram 1.42

- 2 looks low first and then looks for 1 coming off 4's down screen (Diagrams 1.43 and 1.44).

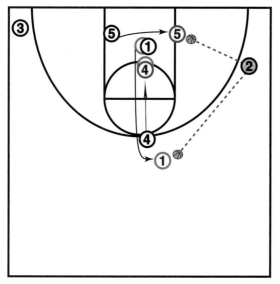

Diagram 1.43

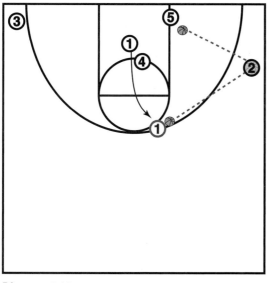

Diagram 1.44

Trail Post Pop Out, After Side Screen

Many teams like to trap screens. Your team must expect this to happen and be prepared to adjust. First, the player being trapped must not panic but stay confident. If possible, he can drag or take an extra dribble to separate himself from the trap. If he doesn't have time to do this, he needs to make one sharp pass out of this trap. This one pass will now give his team a 4 on 3 advantage to attack the basket. Your post player whose defensive man leaves him to trap must now pop out toward the sideline and get ready to receive the pass out of the trap. Your three other players must also read this trap and be ready to flash to the ball, have good spacing, and again get ready to take advantage of the 4 on 3 attack (Diagrams 1.45–1.47).

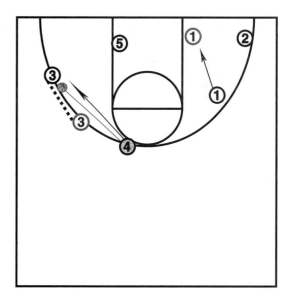

Diagram 1.45

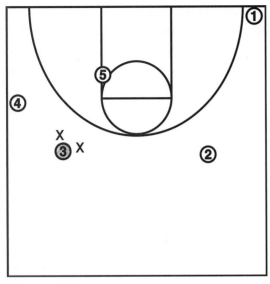

Diagram 1.46

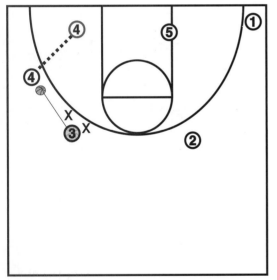

Diagram 1.47

Post Pop Out of Trap

- Should 3 pass to 4, 4 looks to drive the baseline (Diagram 1.48).
- 5 works the middle, 1 is in the corner, and 2 is out on the weak side wing.

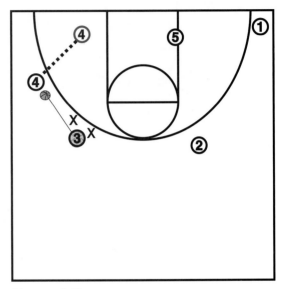

Diagram 1.48

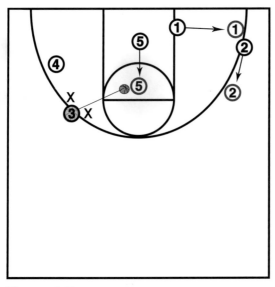

Diagram 1.49

Slip the Screen Should you know that the opposing team is definitely going to trap the 4, 3 ball screen you can have 4 slip the screen. This could be a set play (Diagram 1.51).

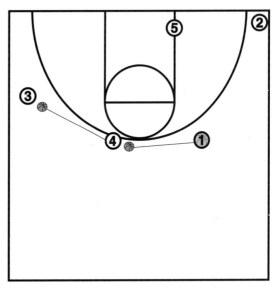

- 5 may have to flash to the middle to receive the pass from 3 (Diagram 1.49).
- 5 then can hit 4 driving to the rim or kick out to either 2 or 1 in the corner (Diagram 1.50).

Diagram 1.51

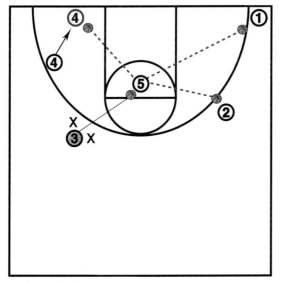

Diagram 1.50

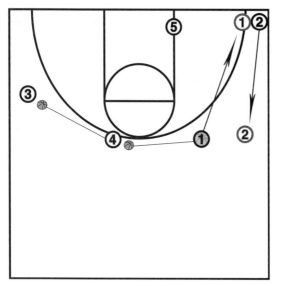

Diagram 1.52

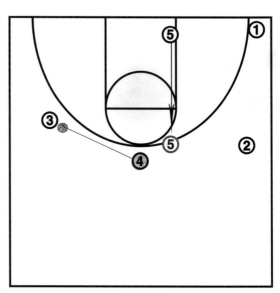

Diagram 1.53

On 1 to 4 pass, 1, instead of going to ball side block like he did before, now interchanges with 2 (Diagram 1.52).

5, instead of following the ball low, now comes high (Diagram 1.53).

On 4 to 3 pass, 4 now slips the screen for an easy layup (Diagram 1.54).

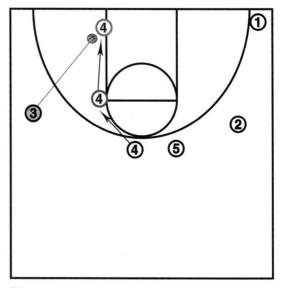

Diagram 1.54

Slip the Screen and Send Opposite Post to Screen on the Ball Should the easy layup to 4 not be there, send 5 to screen on the ball (Diagram 1.55).

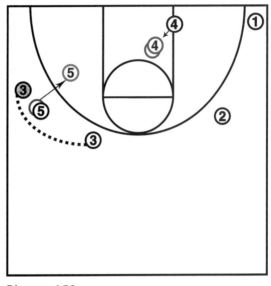

Diagram 1.56

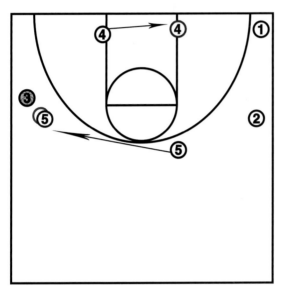

Diagram 1.55

4 goes through to opposite block and gets ready to duck in. 3 uses 5 screen, 5 can roll or pop out, 4 ducks in, 2 and 1 keep spacing and are ready to receive pass from 3 (Diagram 1.56).

I love this look. Lots of good things come from here.

1 Sets the Screen for 5 A little twist for guard through (1-2 pass) is on the 4-2 ball screen. 1 now sets a cross screen for 5 where before 5 set screen for 1. 1 then comes off of 4's down screen (Diagrams 1.57–1.60).

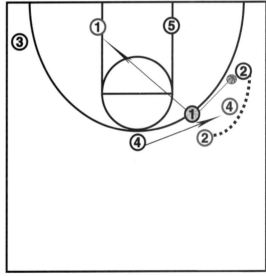

Diagram 1.57

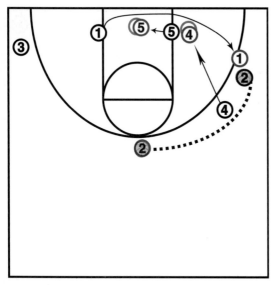

Diagram 1.58

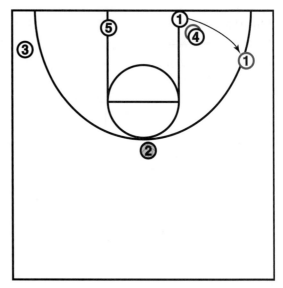

Diagram 1.60

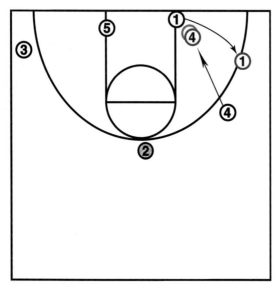

Diagram 1.59

Screen on the Ball

In 1990, when I was coaching at Georgia Tech, we had a very special player in Kenny Anderson. Kenny was so good at using this post trail high screen, it became our main offense. Kenny had great quickness, could score from the perimeter, was an incredible driver of the ball, and was a great passer. He always knew where everybody was on the court. One time against UNC he had 19 assists. It was his finest college moment. I'll talk more about Kenny in Chapter 6.

This screen can seem so simple but can prove incredibly effective. The trail post (4) is always looking to screen the point. He can set a side screen or flat screen.

Once the trail post high screen is set, you can spot up or roll your post. I prefer the spot up where the post steps back or into the open area.

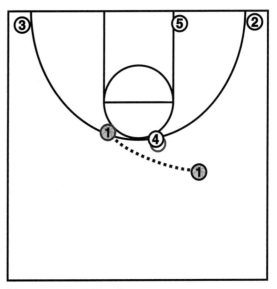

Diagram 1.63 4 Sets Screen

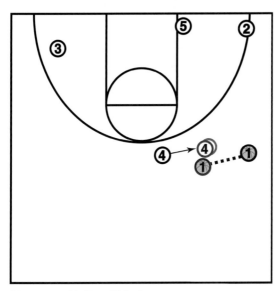

Diagram 1.61 Post Side Screen

Post Spot Up

It's up to 4 to set a great screen and go to the best scoring area. 5 is staying low and always searching for the ball. 2 and 3 are always deep in the corner ready to shoot the 3-ball (Diagrams 1.63 and 1.64).

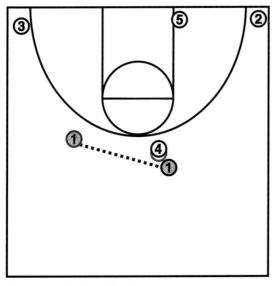

Diagram 1.62 Post Flat Screen

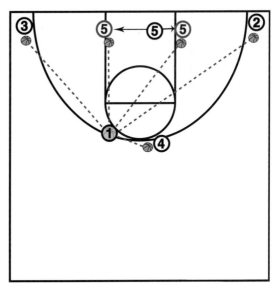

Diagram 1.64 4 Spots Up

Post Roll and Replace. This is also an excellent option.

- 4 sets the screen and rolls to the basket.
- 5, the low post, comes high as 4 rolls (Diagram 1.65).
- 1 is looking for roll post 4 but knows 5 is coming high for a high swing pass (Diagram 1.66).

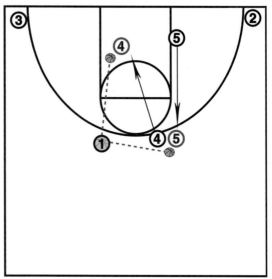

Diagram 1.66

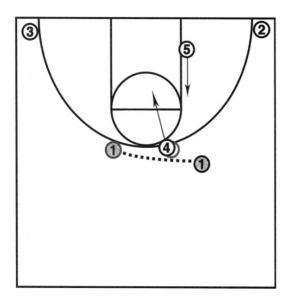

Diagram 1.65

- After using a high screen, 1 can always pass to the ball side wing and you can immediately go to your guard-through action (Diagrams 1.67–1.72) or swing

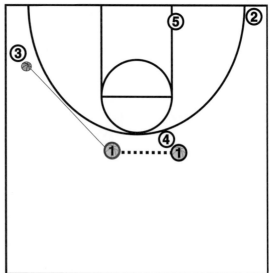

Diagram 1.67 1 to 3 Guard Through

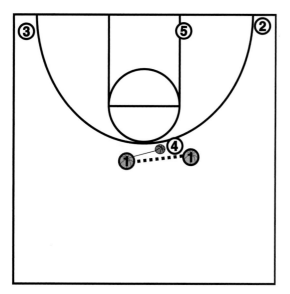

Diagram 1.68 1 Back to 4 Swing Action

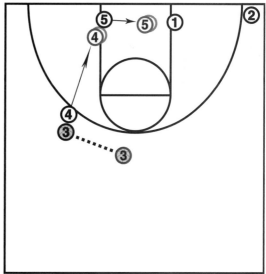

Diagram 1.70

back to the post and go to your swing action (Diagrams 1.73–1.78).

- If 1 passes to the wing, 1 cuts through to the weak side post. 5 follows ball (Diagram 1.69).

- The high post (4) comes over for the high side ball screen (Diagram 1.70).
- 1 will then use the double post staggered screen (Diagrams 1.71 and 1.72).

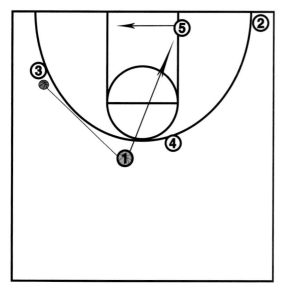

Diagram 1.69

Diagram 1.71

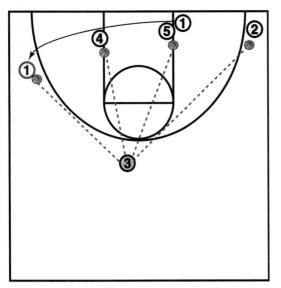

Diagram 1.72

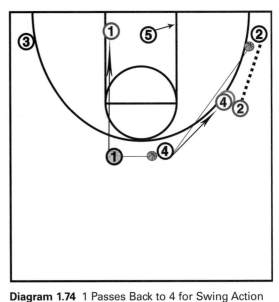

Diagram 1.74 1 Passes Back to 4 for Swing Action

- If 1 passes back to the post, 1 cuts through to the ball side post. On 4's swing pass and screen, 1 will then come off 5 and 4's staggered screens (Diagrams 1.73–1.75).

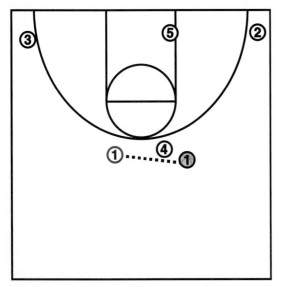

Diagram 1.73 1 Uses 4 High Screen

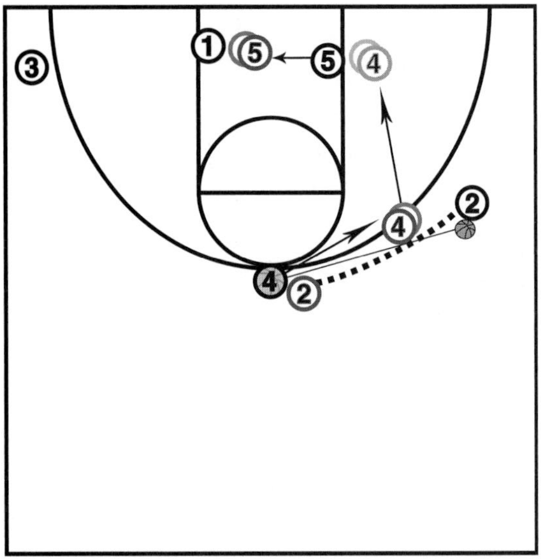

Diagram 1.75

- Like before, we go from 4-out, 1-in to 3-out, 2 (Diagram 1.76).

There are many options from this set.

Point Post

The point (2) passes to the wing (3) and down-screens for the opposite post (4) and then pops out for a pass (Diagrams 1.77 and 1.78).

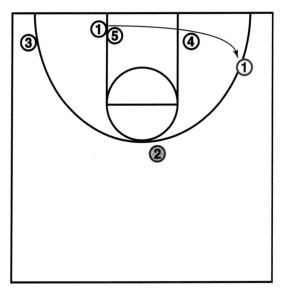

Diagram 1.76

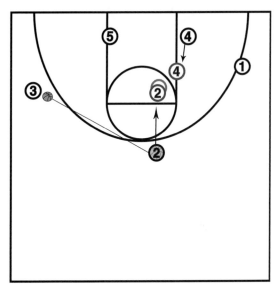

Diagram 1.77

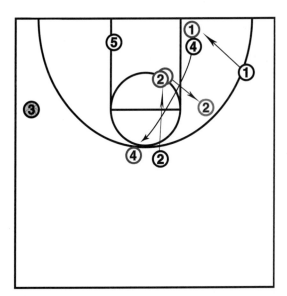

Diagram 1.78

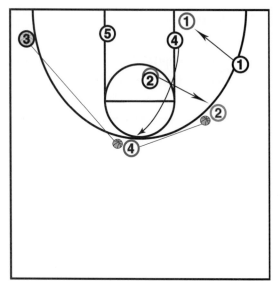

Diagram 1.79

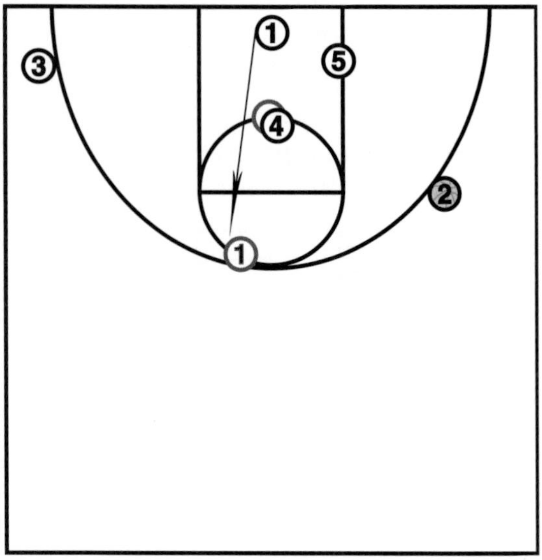

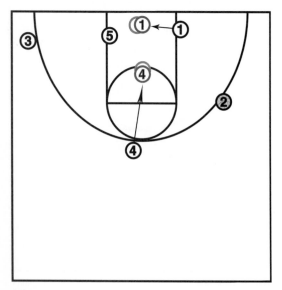

Diagram 1.80

Diagram 1.81

- The opposite wing (1) goes low, and when the point (2) catches the pass from the post (4), 1 will cross-screen low and then use the post's high down screen (Diagrams 1.79–1.81).

Post Pullout

- On the pass to the wing, the ball side post (5) pulls out and screens on the ball.
- 2 cuts through to the weak side.
- 1 comes high (Diagram 1.82).
- 3 uses 5's screen and 5 can roll or pop.
- 4 steps in, and 2 and 1 spot up (Diagram 1.83).

Again, this look can give you great scoring opportunities.

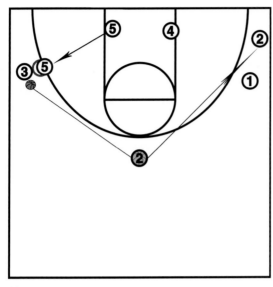

Diagram 1.82

Post Back Screen Point

- On the pass to the wing, opposite post back-screens the point (Diagram 1.84).
- After the post back-screens the point, he can screen on the ball and the point can use a double staggered screen as we did previously (Diagrams 1.85–1.87).

As you can see, there are many options. The key is to know your personnel and use their skills effectively.

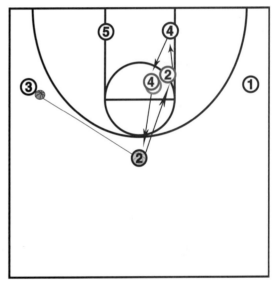

Diagram 1.84

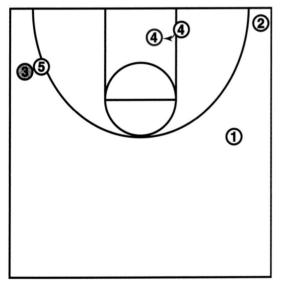

Diagram 1.83

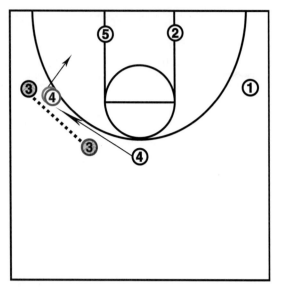

Diagram 1.85

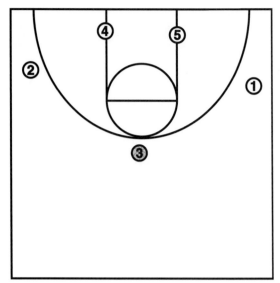

Diagram 1.87

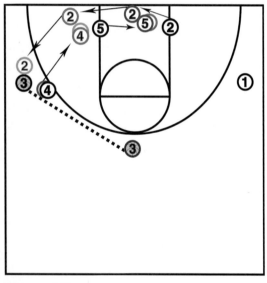

Diagram 1.86

Other Familiar Secondary Looks

Post Swing Pass to Stagger Away

Many teams use this secondary effectively.

- 4 swings to 3.
- 5 isolates low for a pass from 3.
- 1 and 4 stagger away for 2 (Diagrams 1.88–1.90).

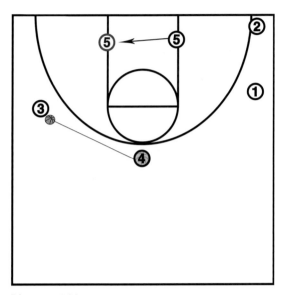

Diagram 1.88

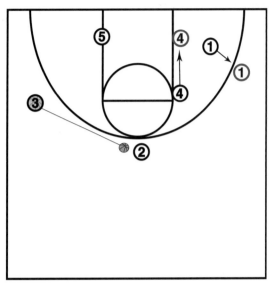

Diagram 1.90

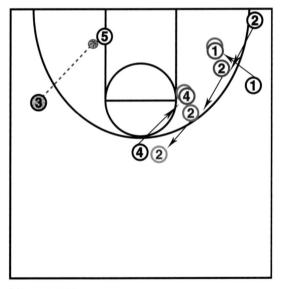

Diagram 1.89

UNC Secondary Most coaches are very familiar with the UNC secondary break. Having coached 19 years against UNC, I watched the legendary Dean Smith and his longtime assistant, Bill Guthridge, make this break very effective. Roy Williams still uses this break with some variations.

- The ball side wing (2) back-screens for the trail post (4) after 4 swing-passes to 3.
- 3 looks low to 5 or can lob for 4 off 2's back screen.
- 2 pops out and you're in 3-out, 2-in motion (Diagrams 191, 192, and 193).

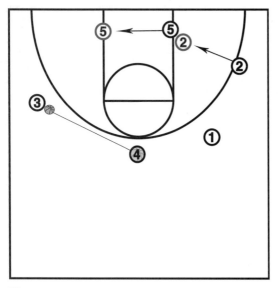

Diagram 1.91

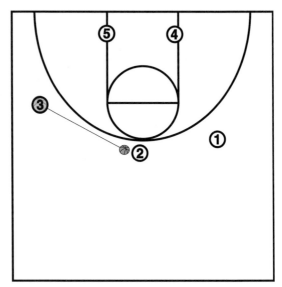

Diagram 1.93

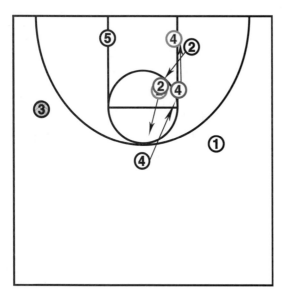

Diagram 1.92

Princeton Offense I'd be remiss not to mention the Princeton offense or variations of it. The 2005 NCAA Tournament was very exciting. West Virginia University's coach, John Beilein, caused plenty of havoc in his team's great run.

I coached against Herb Sendek and later as a TV analyst saw him completely change his system to the Princeton philosophy. Herb has had some great success with this and I could tell how much he enjoyed teaching it. I did a Samford University game and watched Jimmy Tillette's team win and stay very competitive in the Ohio Valley Conference. Samford is now coming to the Southern Conference so we'll see plenty of this offense. The great Pete Carril, former coach of Princeton, now in the NBA, brought this offense to its forefront. But many coaches are now adding to it and making it their own offense. I'm amazed to see the NBA have a few teams running it. It's complicated to learn but very, very difficult to defend. Should you want to explore this offense, I recommend you spend a few days with a coach who runs it.

Speaking of the NBA, how about the Phoenix Suns? They only run to the corners and sides while leaving the middle wide open. Their trail post screens on the ball and rolls to the vacant lane. Of course, they have a very special guard in Steve Nash, but Mike D'Antoni has brought a new and exciting secondary philosophy to the game. New York fans can't wait to see this offense.

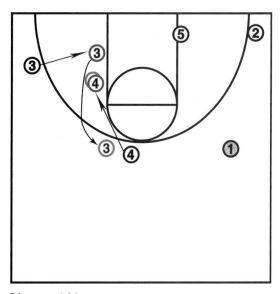

Diagram 1.94

Post Screen Away In this secondary, your trail post will not stop to catch and swing or screen on the ball. Your trail post is now headhunting to screen away for your weak side wing. There were times when our posts were not good at swinging the ball, shooting, or driving the ball. I wish I had gone to this offensive secondary in that case. However, regardless of how well their posts catch and swing, many teams prefer this secondary.

- 3 sets up his defensive man to use the post trail screen by 4 (Diagram 1.94).
- After looking inside for 5, your point (1) dribbles over for a pass to 3.
- On 1's dribble, 2 starts getting ready to go low to baseline to use the 4 down screen after 4 screened for 3 (Diagram 1.95).

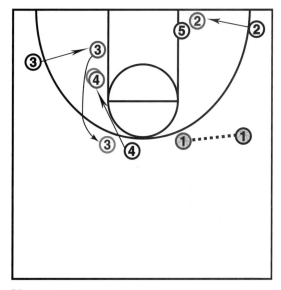

Diagram 1.95

- 5 will come high and on 1 to 3 pass. 4 continues low to screen 2 while 5 comes high to flair screen for 1. 3 has the ball and now becomes your point guard with lots of passing options (Diagram 1.96).
- When 3 catches the pass from 1, he looks low for 5 and then 2 coming off the second post down screen set by 4.
- 3 can also look to 1 coming off 5's flair screen or swing pass to 5. 5 can always go and set a ball screen for 3. This look gives you lots of options.

Swing Wing Deny
Wrap Around Option

- Should the weak side wing (3) ever be denied, he wraps around 4 looking for a pass from 1 (Diagram 1.97).
- Should 1 not pass to 3, he continues his dribble and looks for 2 coming off 4's down screen (Diagram 1.98).

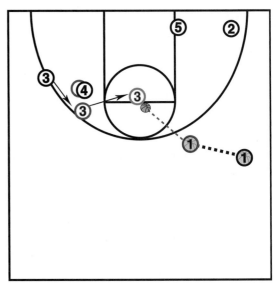

Diagram 1.97

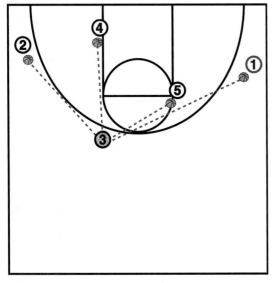

Diagram 1.96

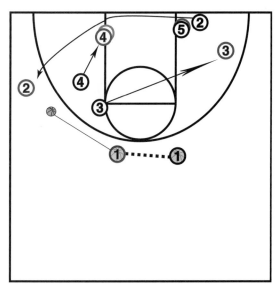

Diagram 1.98

As you can see, there are many fast-break options. Make your choice and stick with it. Options you never thought of will happen, and players will learn exactly where to run to, understand deny options, and have lots of fun executing them. You want up-tempo basketball with precise passing and movement. I call it "free-flowing offense."

We now move on to the missed-shot break. No one loves this more than Duke's Mike Krzyzewski.

MISSED-SHOT BREAK

What's great about this break is that your defense forced the opponent to miss or turn over the ball. The key to this break is simply running lanes. The missed-shot break can seem disorganized at times, but in reality it adheres to many principles in the made-shot break. Remember, whatever your post trail rule is—to catch or screen away—it's the same on the missed-shot break.

With the missed-shot break, I allow our 4 and sometimes our 5 man to take the middle (point) lane. I prefer they take a few dribbles and get it to a guard as soon as they can. I like this because it causes more unpredictability on the break. However, whether you allow your 2, 3, 4, or 5 man to take the middle lane on a missed shot is totally up to you. The University of Florida's great coach, Billy Donovan, allowed 6-foot, 11-inch Joakim Noah to start the break if he rebounded the ball.

4 Rebounds, Multiple-Lane Break

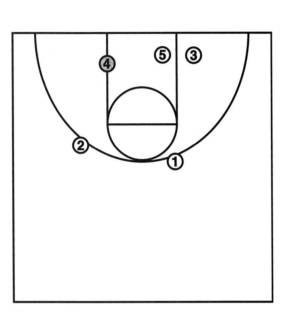

Diagram 1.99

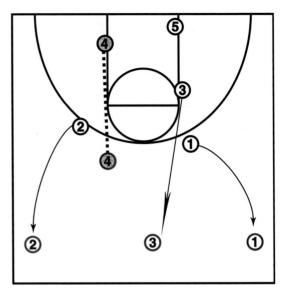

Diagram 1.100

Let's say 4 rebounds, and since he's a good ball handler you allow him to take the point lane (Diagram 1.99).

Now 3 takes the first post lane, 2 and 1 take the wing lanes, and 5 takes the trail post lane (Diagram 1.100).

- 4 declares ball side and, being the point guard, must do exactly what 1 would do.
- 3 posts up ball side and 4 makes a swing pass to 5 (Diagram 1.101).
- 5 swings to 1 or if necessary dribbles hands off with 1. Should he pass to 1, 1 looks low to 3 following the ball.

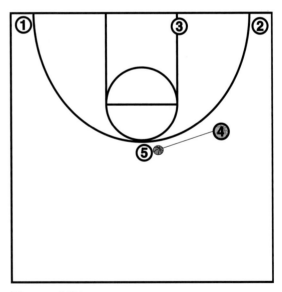

Diagram 1.101

5 follows pass and sets ball screen for 1. 4 dives low and 2 pushes up (Diagram 1.102).

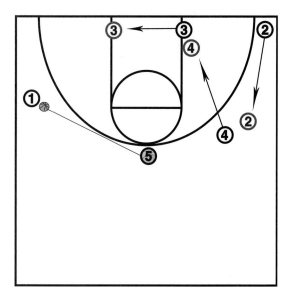

Diagram 1.102

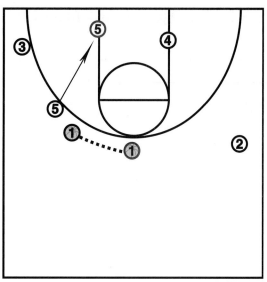

Diagram 1.104

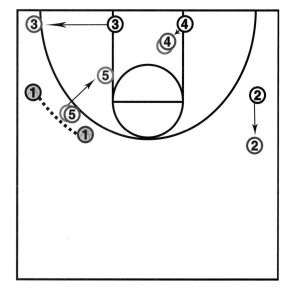

Diagram 1.103

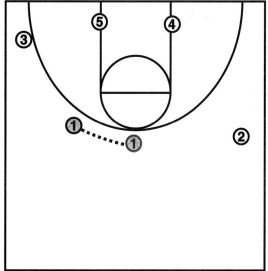

Diagram 1.105

- 3, after posting up, will pop out to corner when 5 screens for 1. 4 ducks in, 2 spaces out, and 5 rolls after setting ball screen for 1 (Diagrams 1.103 and 1.104).

This is great action and you're back to your 3-out, 2-in look (Diagram 1.105).

4 Swings to Ball Side Wing Option

4, instead of swinging the ball, passes to the ball side wing (Diagram 1.106).

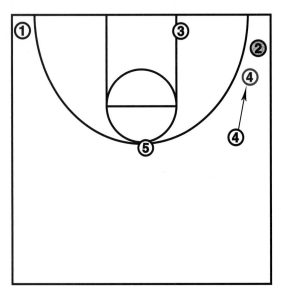

Diagram 1.106

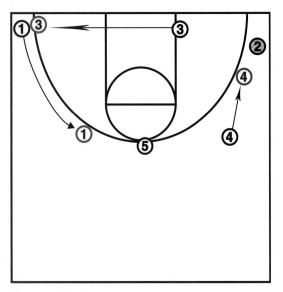

Diagram 1.107

3 can still momentarily post up. But as 4 follows his pass to 2 and begins to set a ball screen for 2, 3 will clear to the weak side corner (Diagram 1.107)

You now have a great miss shot break look that gives you great scoring opportunities (Diagram 1.108).

4 can roll or pop. Remember, you can do this on either side.

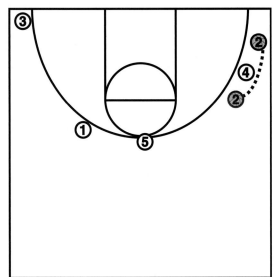

Diagram 1.108

3 Rebounds

Now let's say 3 gets the rebound and takes the middle lane on his side (Diagram 1.109):

- 1 and 2 will fill the outside lanes.
- 5 takes the middle rim lane and 4 will take the trail post lane (Diagrams 1.110 and 1.111).

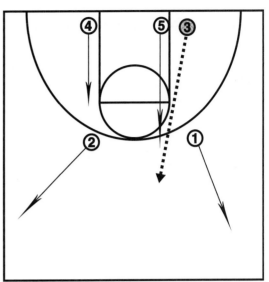

Diagram 1.110

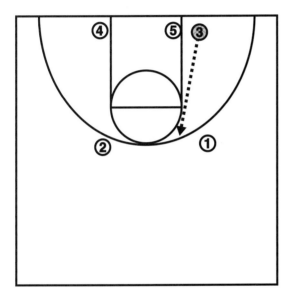

Diagram 1.109

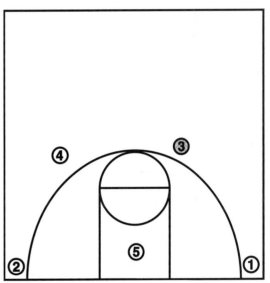

Diagram 1.111

Should 3 pass to 1, you can run the guard-through series (Diagram 1.112).

1 looks to 5 posting up on ball side. 4 comes over to ball screen on 1 and you're in it (Diagram 1.113).

Should 3 pass to 4 you're in your swing series (Diagram 1.114).

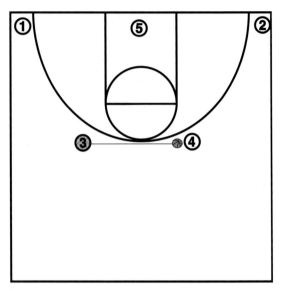

Diagram 1.114

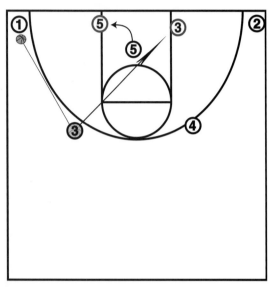

Diagram 1.112

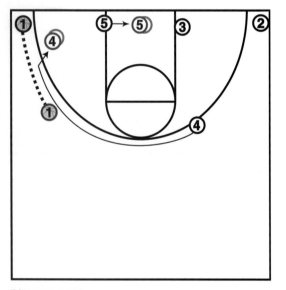

Diagram 1.113

5 follows the ball, 3 cuts ball side block, 4 looks high low to 5 then swings to 2, follows his pass to set ball screen for 2, and you're in it (Diagrams 1.115 and 1.116).

Hopefully you are getting the idea.

The fun and exciting aspect of this break is its unpredictability. It can't be scouted and it is difficult to defend.

Your players will come to love it, and it should make them want to play better defense.

The better the defense, the more missed-shot breaks.

In 1990, Kenny Anderson initially had trouble with this break. Kenny was so accustomed to having the ball in his hands, he would forget to fill a lane and get left behind. Kenny eventually caught on and was on the receiving end of some pretty good passes.

Remember that with continued practice of this break your players will eventually get it and your team will be off and running.

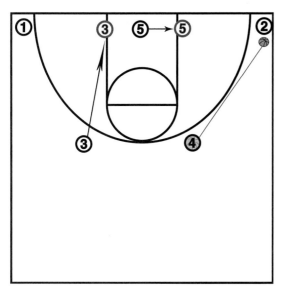

Diagram 1.115

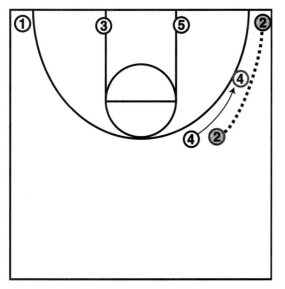

Diagram 1.116

CHAPTER 2

Attacking the Pressure

After teaching the made and missed-shot breaks, we now go right into teaching offense versus pressure defenses. Many coaches today love pressure defense. While I was at Georgia Tech, we had the pleasure of facing UNC with Dean Smith's full-court man-to-man run-and-jump, Maryland with Gary Williams's full-court and three-quarter-court diamond press, and Duke with Mike Krzyzewski's half-court denying passing lanes and baseline traps.

Outside the ACC, Tubby Smith's University of Georgia and Kentucky teams along with Rick Pitino's Kentucky and now Louisville teams always made their pressing defenses a very tough challenge. The University of Tennessee's Bruce Pearl has completely rejuvenated Volunteer basketball with his full-court pressing philosophy.

Offensively, you must expect and be prepared for pressure and have the mind-set that you love seeing pressure and, in planning to attack pressure, you expect to get some great looks, including open 3s and dunks. In other words, you are not going to let pressure bother you. Easier said than done, but we'll go over different ways to attack pressure and hopefully avoid those bad turnovers that lead to easy baskets for the opponents.

We have two types of pressure attacks: live and dead-ball looks.

LIVE ATTACKS: ATTACKING FULL-COURT PRESSURE FROM A REGULAR FAST-BREAK LOOK

Attacking pressure in this look continues to give your point guard plenty of room to get open. Your ball side wing (2) and your weak side wing (3) must be ready to come back to the baseline to receive the pass from 4. 5 continues to run the rim lane and, unless necessary, is not involved with the initial pressure break. Again, giving 1 plenty of space is very important. 1 must use his quickness to get open (Diagram 2.1).

Short Corner 4-1 Pass

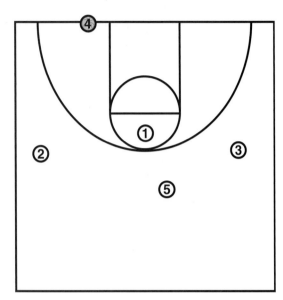

Diagram 2.1

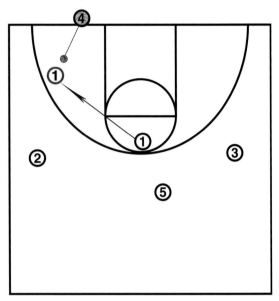

Diagram 2.2

Should 4 pass to 1 in the short corner, 4 will immediately step in behind 1 as an outlet for 1. 2 is 1's ball side outlet, 3 is the weak side and middle flash outlet, while 5 is the weak side long (Diagrams 2.2 and 2.3).

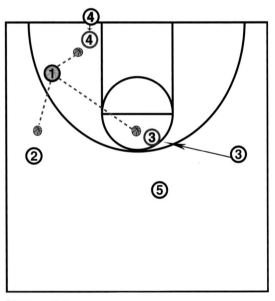

Diagram 2.3

1-2 Sideline Pass

Should 1 pass to 2, 2 can hit 3 (the middle flasher), break the press himself to the middle or sideline, or if necessary go back to 1 (Diagram 2.4).

Should 1 pass back to your inbounder (4), 3 gets back to the weak side sideline while the pass is in the air. 1 and 2 hold while 4 saddle-dribbles toward 3 (Diagrams 2.5 and 2.6).

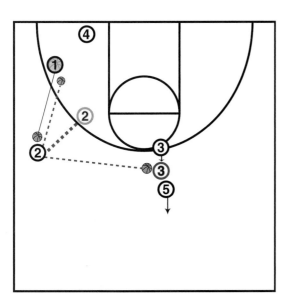

Diagram 2.4

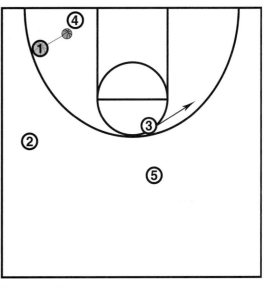

Diagram 2.5

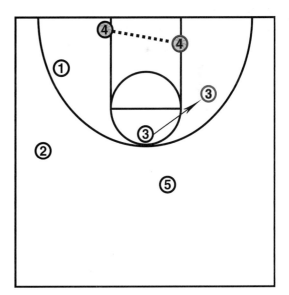

Diagram 2.6

On 4's pass to 3, 1 flashes to the middle, 4 stays behind the ball, 2 is weak side, and 5 can work sideline long (Diagram 2.7).

3, like 2, can hit 1 coming to the middle or break the pressure himself (Diagrams 2.8 and 2.9).

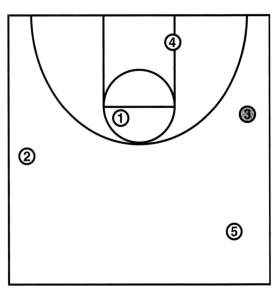

Diagram 2.8

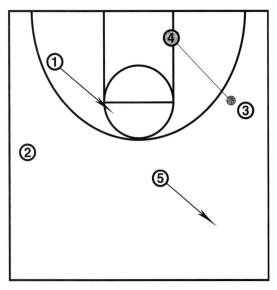

Diagram 2.7

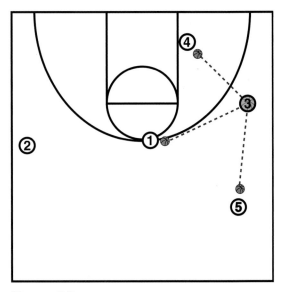

Diagram 2.9

Long Corner 4-1 Pass

1 cuts hard to the long corner to receive the pass (Diagram 2.10).

Again, 4 steps in behind the ball, 3 is now the ball side outlet, and 2 is your weak side middle flasher. The same principles apply as in the short corner 4-1 pass (Diagram 2.11).

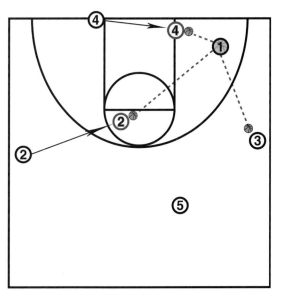

Diagram 2.10

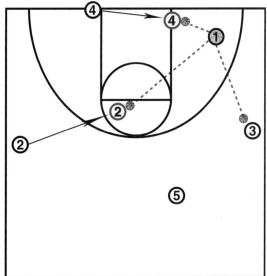

Diagram 2.11

4 Pass to Wings

1 is denied the initial pass, so now 2 and 3 must come back hard to the ball. After a made basket, 4 is allowed to run the baseline (Diagram 2.12).

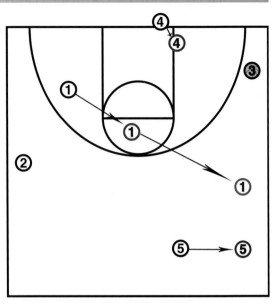

Diagram 2.13

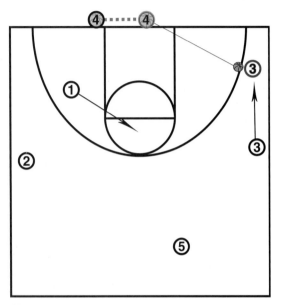

Diagram 2.12

On this pass, 1 works the middle and ball side sideline, 4 stays behind the ball, 2 is weak side, and 5 can work sideline long (Diagram 2.13).

4-2 Initial Pass

Again, 1 is denied the first pass, so now 2 comes back hard to receive the pass from 4 (Diagram 2.14).

Again, 1 works the middle and ball side sideline, 4 stays behind the ball, 3 is weak side, and 5 is long weak side (Diagram 2.15).

It's very important for 1 to keep moving and trying to get open when he is being denied. He should never stop moving or cutting. This will get him open or one of the wings.

Practicing live ball a lot, using the regular fast-break look versus pressure, is very important. You'll see who can get open to receive the

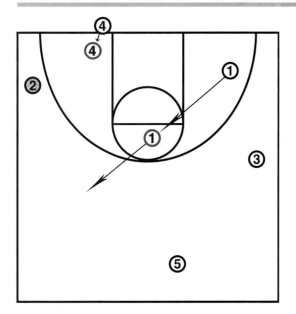

Diagram 2.14

Should you be having trouble inbounding the ball from the regular fast-break look, you have two other choices: screening, or going to your dead-ball look where a wing inbounds the ball rather than your posts.

Screening

There are many options for screening to get someone open.

1 screens for 3 and comes back hard to the ball (Diagrams 2.16 and 2.17).

pass, where the outlets will be, and who has the courage to make passes or dribble to get easy shots.

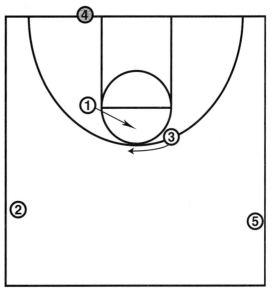

Diagram 2.16

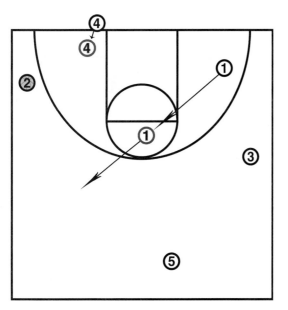

Diagram 2.15

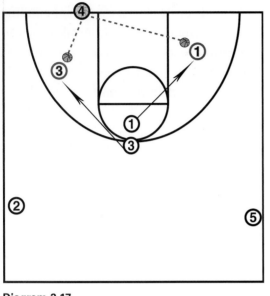

Diagram 2.17

Should 4 pass to 1, 2 now works the middle, 5 is ball side outlet, 4 steps in behind, and 3 slides up to become weak side outlet (Diagrams 2.19 and 2.20).

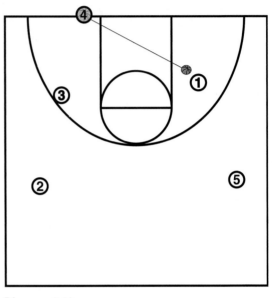

Diagram 2.19

Once the ball is inbounded, the same outlet rules apply. On 4 to 3 pass, 2 stays ball side, 1 works the middle, 4 steps in behind, and 5 works long on the weak side (Diagram 2.18).

Diagram 2.18

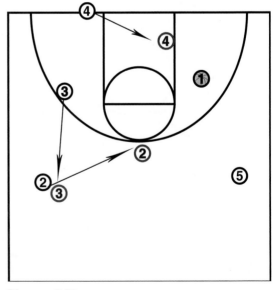

Diagram 2.20

Its not a bad idea to bring 5 back and have him screen for 1 (Diagram 2.21).

5, after screening for 1, will work the middle. 2 and 3 are ready to work the sidelines (Diagram 2.22).

Should 4 pass to 5, he's looking for a quick outlet pass to 2, 3, or back to 1 (Diagram 2.23).

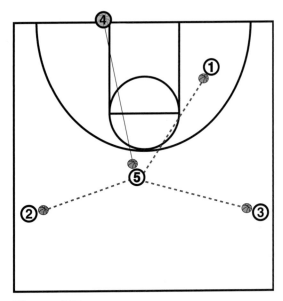

Diagram 2.23

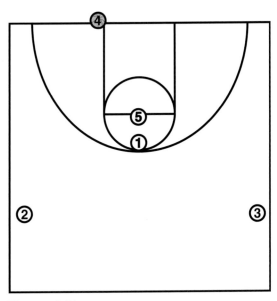

Diagram 2.21

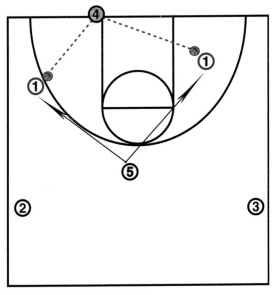

Diagram 2.22

Should 1 ever pass back to 4, 5 runs rim, 1 works the middle, and 2 and 3 work the sidelines (Diagram 2.24).

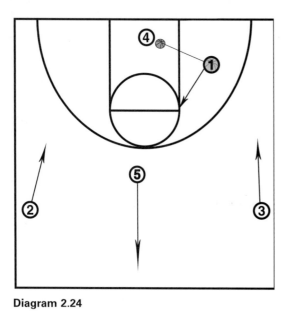

Diagram 2.24

Sometimes 1 can back-screen for 5 to go long. After setting screen, 1 comes back to the ball. 2 and 3 work the sidelines (Diagram 2.25).

4 can throw long to 5, short to 1, or sideline to 2 or 3.

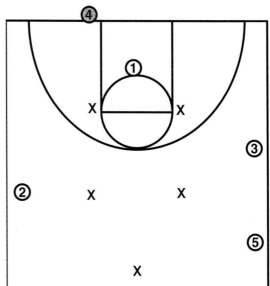

Diagram 2.25

DEAD-BALL LOOK

We use this look after free throws, in late-game situations, after time-outs, when we are being pressed the entire game, or when our regular fast break is not working. A wing (2 or 3) will inbound the ball. Let's pick 3.

You can do a lot of things similar to what we did when 4 inbounded the ball (Diagrams 2.26 and 2.27).

Study your personnel and experiment with them. Do what fits your personnel and what gets the job done.

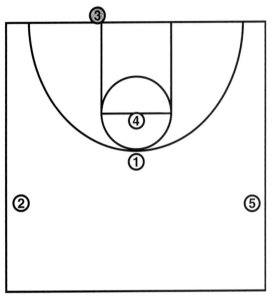

Diagram 2.27

Attacking Three-Quarter Court Pressure from a Regular Fast-Break Look

Now your opponent allows you to inbound the ball, take away the middle, and force some traps in certain areas. A popular press to do this is the 2-2-1 or the 1-2-2.

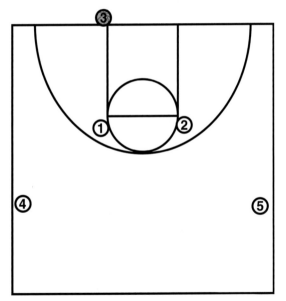

Diagram 2.26

2-2-1

4 inbounds to 1 and then goes sideline on 2's side. 2 pushes to middle and we attack in a 1-3-1 look (Diagrams 2.28 and 2.29).

1-2-2

This is another popular three-quarter court press. 4 will inbound to 1, and now stays even or slightly behind 1. 5 now works middle and 2 and 3 go deep to the corners (Diagram 2.30).

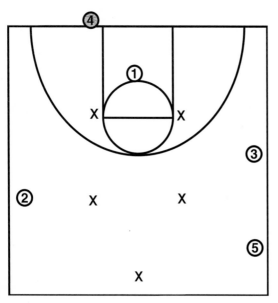

Diagram 2.28

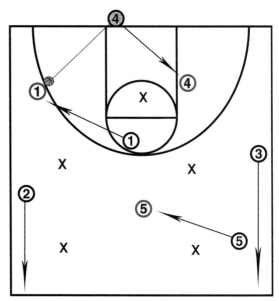

Diagram 2.30

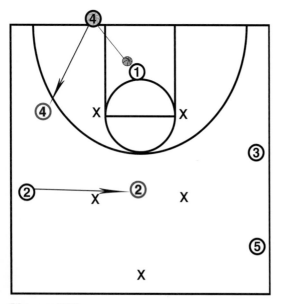

Diagram 2.29

As you can see, we're now trying to have a one-man front versus the 2-2-1.

Scouting opponents allows you to prepare for different types of pressure. Again, by practicing a lot against different pressure sets, you will see what's best for your team.

Regardless of what pressure we face, I want our players to always have the mind-set to attack. The person inbounding the ball should be one of your smarter players. The players receiving the ball need courage and outlets. Once you feel you have the advantage, attack and get the high-percentage shot. Should you get caught off-guard, a quick time-out is a lot better than a turnover. Sometimes have your starting point guard foul out and see how your team reacts. It happens more than you can imagine.

Losing a lead because a team suddenly pressures can really hurt. Work hard on late-game situations and be prepared to close the deal. I always keep a few special plays versus pressure for late-game situations. Chapter 5 covers special situations that will include these plays.

CHAPTER 3

Transition to Half-Court Basketball

There are times when you have your running game going but you're either not scoring or your key people are not touching the ball. This means it's time to run your bread-and-butter plays and play some half-court basketball. To do this, you need to have "go-to" plays that will deliver a key basket and get the momentum back in your direction.

A good example of this would be Roy Williams's UNC 2004 national champions. Roy absolutely loves the running game and does it as well or better than anyone coaching today. UNC's 2004 team had Raymond Felton's speed and passing along with Sean May's running and catching, making their running game unbelievable at times. However, Roy, like Bill Guthridge and Dean Smith before him, had an excellent half-court set to deliver key baskets when they needed them. I believe these sets play an important part of a team's offensive scheme.

How many of these plays you want is entirely up to you and your philosophy. You can do different plays off your secondary break or again have plays from different sets. These plays can get you some great looks for your best scoring players. I'll put a couple of these plays in early and then add some more as the season progresses. I am always looking for new plays and pick some up watching other teams and even watching the NBA. Many coaches refer to these plays as their "go-to" plays. Since I already talked about UNC, let's go over one of their box sets that I also use at the College of Charleston. It's very good to us.

BOX SET

- 5 and 4 pop out. 1 can hit either, but it's better that the superior offensive post receive the first pass (Diagram 3.1).

- On that pass, the ball side wing (2) pops out to the corner (Diagram 3.2).
- The weak side wing (3) replaces 2 and posts up (first option) (Diagram 3.3).

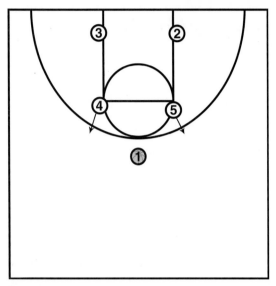

Diagram 3.1

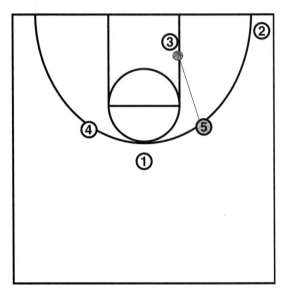

Diagram 3.3

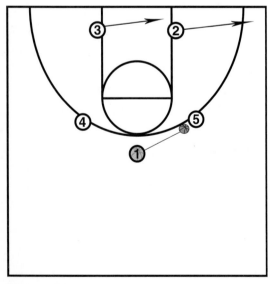

Diagram 3.2

- Simultaneously, 4 back-screens for 1 and pops to the ball (Diagrams 3.4 and 3.5).

- 5, after looking at 3 post up, also has the option to reverse to 4 (5 can throw a skip pass to 1 if he's open) (Diagram 3.6).
- On the reverse pass, 3 steps up and back-screens for 5.
- 4 reverses to 1 (Diagram 3.7).

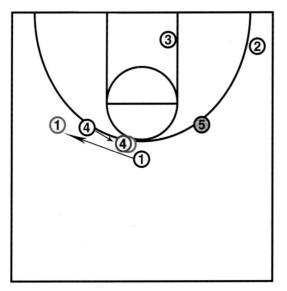

Diagram 3.4

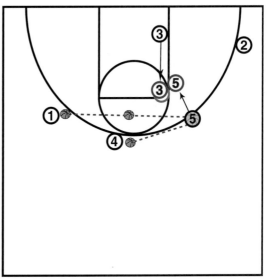

Diagram 3.6

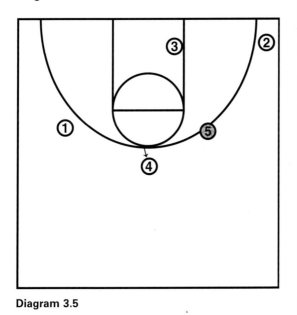

Diagram 3.5

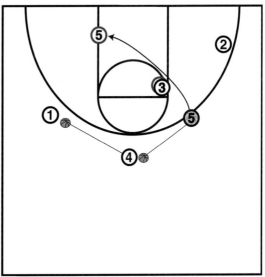

Diagram 3.7

- Should 1 be denied, the backdoor cut is wide open. After 4 reverses the ball, he will screen the screener, 3 (Diagram 3.8).
- 1's first option is looking for 5 coming off 3's back screen. 1's second option is looking for 3 coming off 4's screen (Diagram 3.9).

Many times Sean May came off that back screen and scored low, or Rashad McCants, who set the back screen, came off 5's screen for a big 3. Again, you can run this play from either side.

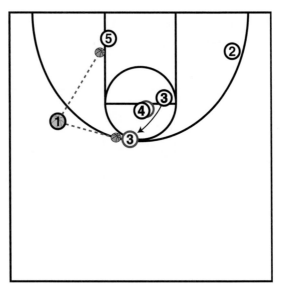

Diagram 3.9

SECONDARY LOOK

This is what I call going to your half-court offense from your secondary game, and I believe it's a great complement to the running game.

Post Trail (4)

- 4 screens away for 3 and pops out (Diagram 3.10).
- 3 wraps around 4's screen and posts up. 1 passes to 4 (Diagram 3.11).
- While the 4 and 3 screens are taking place, 5 and 2 slide up to foul line extended (Diagram 3.12).
- On the 1 to 4 pass, 1 cuts hard to the basket and will pop out to the weak side wing.

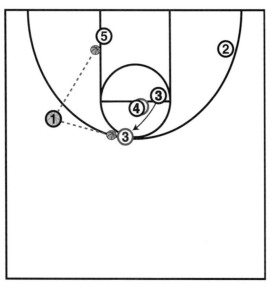

Diagram 3.8

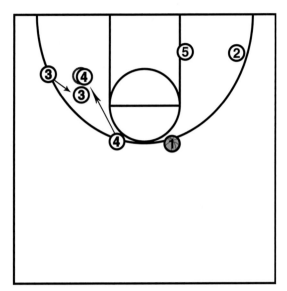

Diagram 3.10

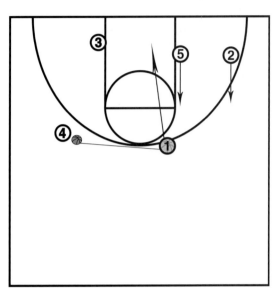

Diagram 3.12

- 2 wraps around 5's screen at the elbow looking for a pass from 4.
- 5 pops out after 2 wraps around him.

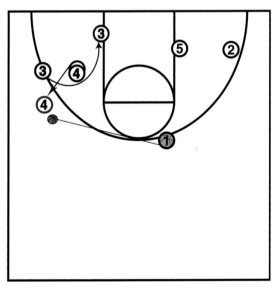

Diagram 3.11

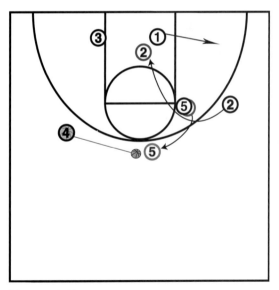

Diagram 3.13

- 4 looks for 3 posting up, looks for 2 cutting, and then reverses to 5 (Diagram 3.13).

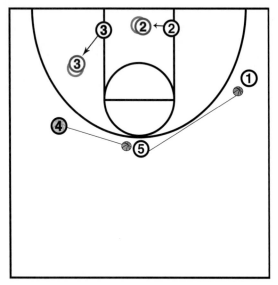

Diagram 3.14

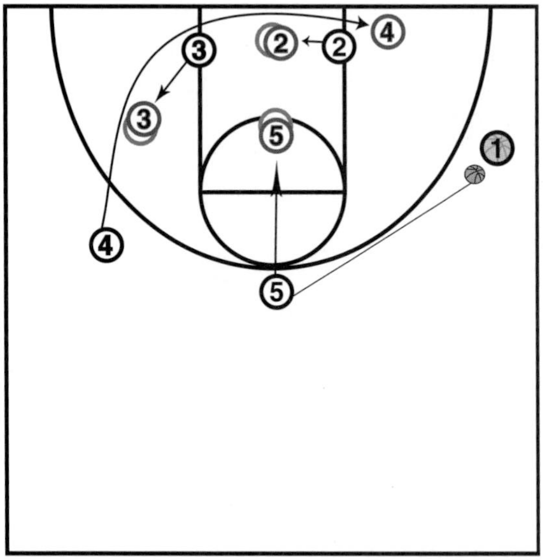

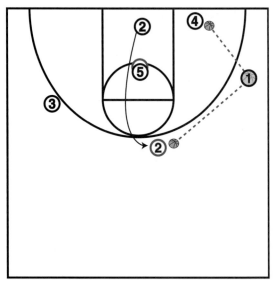

Diagram 3.15

- On the 4 to 5 pass, 3 and 2 will set staggered screens for 4 and 5 reverses to 1 (Diagram 3.14).
- After reversing to 1, 5 screens down for 2 (Diagram 3.15).
- 1 looks for 4 coming off the double staggered screen (he's usually open) or reverses to 2 coming off 5's down screen for an open shot (Diagram 3.16).
- Should 4's defensive man try to short-cut the play, you could throw a lob pass to 4.

Diagram 3.16

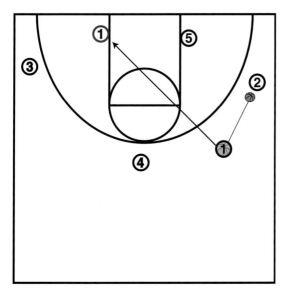

Diagram 3.17

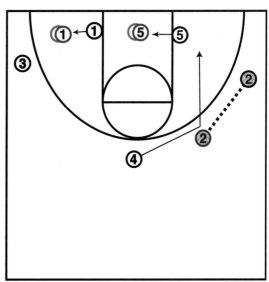

Diagram 3.18

Triple Screen

Another play we like off our secondary look is setting a triple screen for our weak side wing.

- 1 passes to 2 and, like he always does, cuts to the weak side box (Diagram 3.17).
- 4 comes over to ball-screen for 2 but instead will slip the screen (Diagram 3.18).
- Once 4 slips the screen, your weak side wing (3) will use 1, 5, and 4's screen.
- 2 will dribble toward the middle and look for 3 coming off the triple staggered screen (Diagrams 3.19 and 3.20).

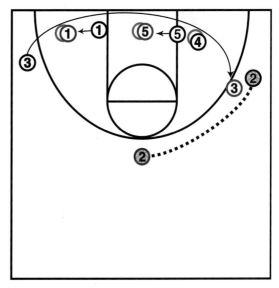

Diagram 3.19

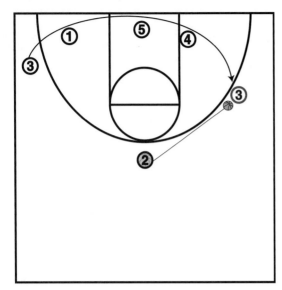

Diagram 3.20

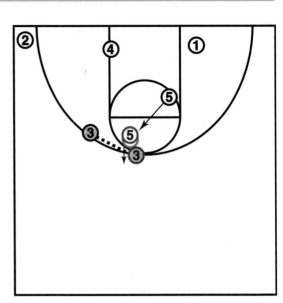

Diagram 3.21

LOB PLAY

Every coach has a lob play to deliver a big basket. We used this for Stephon Marbury a few times, since Stephon was so athletic.

Break Look

- 4 goes hard to the basket.
- 5 steps up.
- 3 comes back hard to the ball.
- 2 goes to the opposite corner off 4.
- 1 dribbles to the middle for pass to 3 (Diagram 3.21).
- 5 sets a UCLA back screen for 1.
- 3 is now the point guard and looks for a lob to 1 (Diagrams 3.22 and 3.23).
- If defense goes below the screen, 1 can

flare back looking for the pass to drive or shoot 3 may need to dribble and pass to 1 (Diagram 3.24).

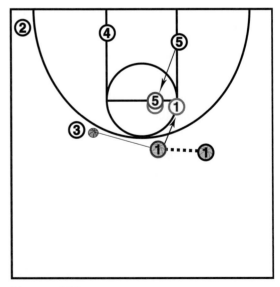

Diagram 3.22

- If the lob is not there, 5 immediately ball-screens for 3 (Diagram 3.25).
- 1 pops to corner. 3 uses 5's ball-screen (Diagram 3.26).

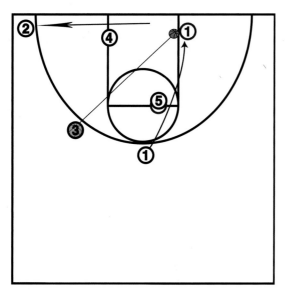

Diagram 3.23

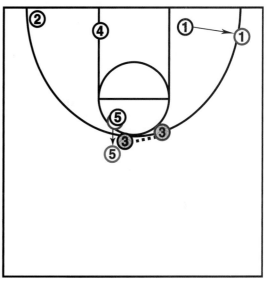

Diagram 3.25

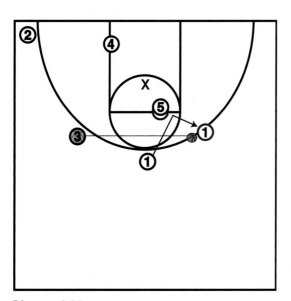

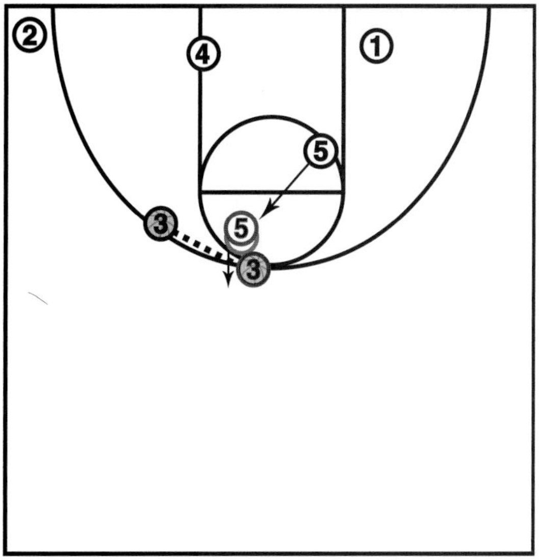

Diagram 3.24

Diagram 3.26

BACKDOOR PLAY

You always need a good backdoor play versus hard man-to-man pressure.

- Have 4 screen away for the weak side wing 3 (Diagram 3.27).
- 4 continues low to screen for 2 coming to the opposite corner.
- 1 passes to 3.
- 5 comes up and flare-screens for 1 (Diagram 3.28).
- 3 passes to 5 and interchanges with 2.
- 4 steps up (Diagram 3.29).

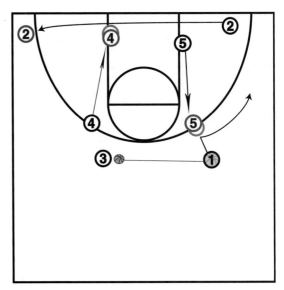

Diagram 3.28

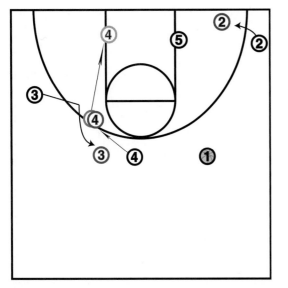

Diagram 3.27

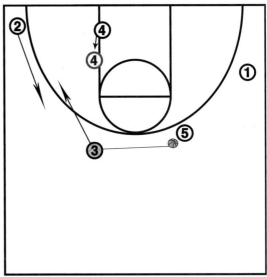

Diagram 3.29

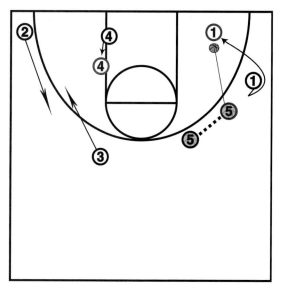

Diagram 3.30

Diagram 3.31

- 5 dribbles hard at 1. Then 1 starts for a dribble handoff but instead goes backdoor (Diagram 3.30).

POST BACK SCREEN OUT OF SECONDARY

This is another great set out of your secondary look.

- 1 passes to 2 and uses a high flare screen set by 4 (Diagram 3.31).
- Your weak side wing (3) will now come ball side off 5 (Diagram 3.32).
- 2's first look is to 5. 2 then swings to 4 who swings to 1. If 1 is denied, he can go backdoor on a 4 to 1 pass.
- 5 sets the back screen for 2.
- 3 goes low nearer to block.

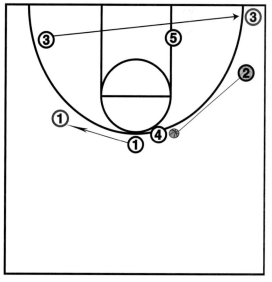

Diagram 3.32

- 4 passes to 1 (Diagram 3.33).
- 1 looks for 2 coming off 5's back screen.
- After 5 back-screens, he screens for 3. 3 comes off 5 and 4's staggered screen (Diagrams 3.34 and 3.35).

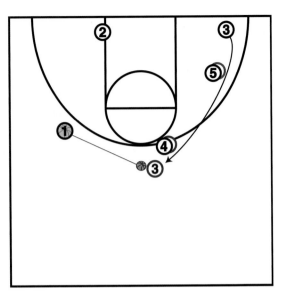

Diagram 3.35

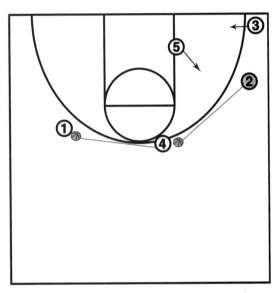

Diagram 3.33

- 1 passes to 3. When 3 catches the ball, 2 will use another 5 and 4 staggered screen and look to receive the ball from 3 (Diagram 3.36).

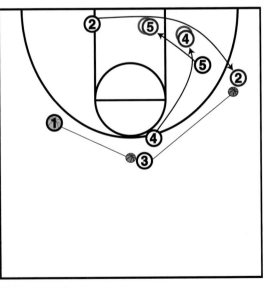

Diagram 3.36

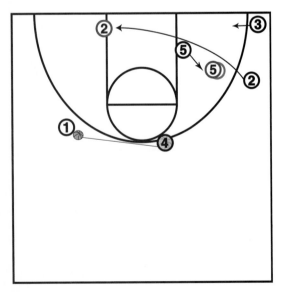

Diagram 3.34

STACKS SET

- 2 and 3 go to the blocks. 5 sets behind 3 while 4 sets behind 2 (Diagram 3.37).
- 2 triggers this set by coming off the double screen by 3 and 4 (Diagram 3.38).

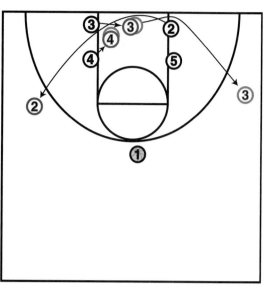

Diagram 3.38

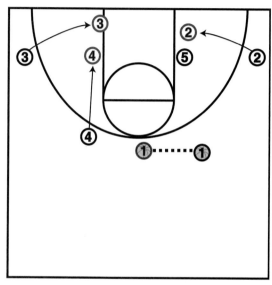

Diagram 3.37

- 3 goes opposite 2.
- 1 has the choice of passing to 2 or 3 (Diagram 3.39).

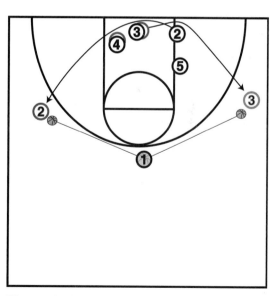

Diagram 3.39

I think you're getting the idea of how important some, if not many, bread-and-butter plays can be. You must have these plays down pat and execute them precisely. The half-court plays from this chapter will not only give the defense different looks, but they will also give your running game balance and versatility.

CHAPTER 4

Zone Offense

Obviously, many teams will play zone defense throughout the game to disrupt your offensive flow. Today's best zone coach has to be Jim Boeheim. It's his primary defense and Jim totally believes in it.

Another Hall of Fame coach, John Chaney, gave me and many others fits with his zone defense. You cannot allow a team to simply go zone and stop your offensive attack. You have to have a zone attack that allows your team to continue their offensive attack.

There are many zone offenses. You need to study as many as possible until you find the one you're most comfortable teaching. You see many different defensive zones, but whether it's a 2-3, 3-2, or 1-3-1, your team must continue to attack and maintain your offensive attack.

VERSUS 2-3 ZONES

Let's start by attacking the most common zone, the 2-3. I got this offense from watching another team run it and I always like to tweak it and add something to it.

Screen on Ball, Corner Attack

- 1 dribbles at 2. 2 slides across and above the foul line to the weak side wing.
- The ball side post (5) slides up to screen for 1.
- 4 slides low and 3 stays in the corner (Diagram 4.1).

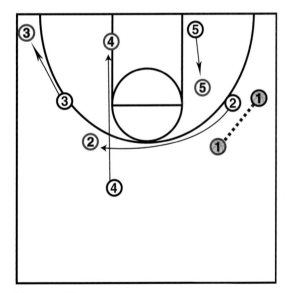

Diagram 4.1

71

- 1 uses 5's screen and 5 pops out or rolls low.
- 4 ducks in (Diagram 4.2).
- 1 swings to 2, who looks low to 4 and swings to 3 (Diagram 4.3).
- 4 follows the ball and posts up, always looking for the pass to post (Diagram 4.4).

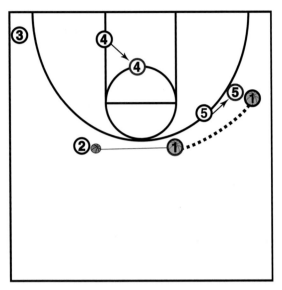

Diagram 4.3

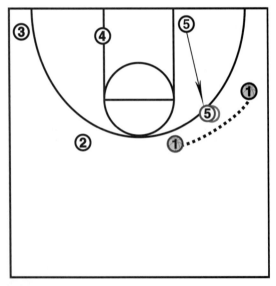

Diagram 4.2

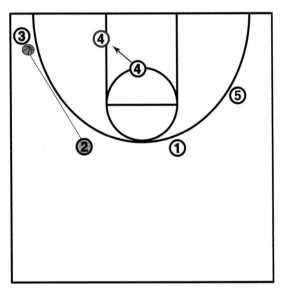

Diagram 4.4

- 3 looks low to 4, then swings back to 2.
- 3 starts going to the opposite corner.
- 4 slides up to set a screen for 2 and 5 slides low (Diagram 4.5).
- 5 ducks in and 1 slides over (Diagram 4.6).
- After screening for 2, 4 pops out or rolls.
- 2 hits 1, who looks low to 5 and swings to 3 (Diagram 4.7).

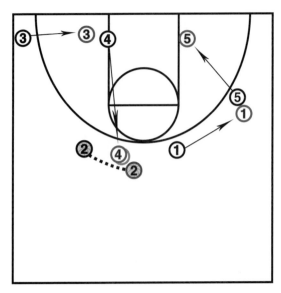

Diagram 4.6

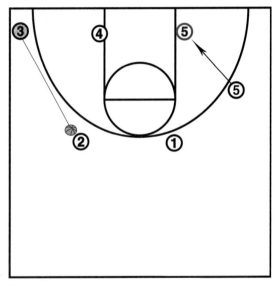

Diagram 4.5

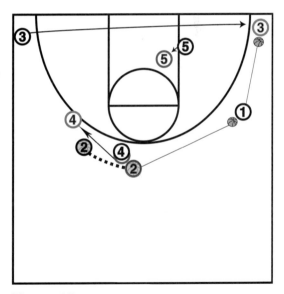

Diagram 4.7

- 3 looks low to 5, swings back to 1, and goes to the opposite corner (Diagram 4.8).
- 5 slides up to screen for 1.

- 4 slides low to the opposite block, bringing the play full circle and allowing you to continue the continuity (Diagrams 4.9–4.11).

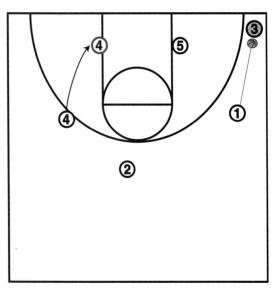

Diagram 4.8

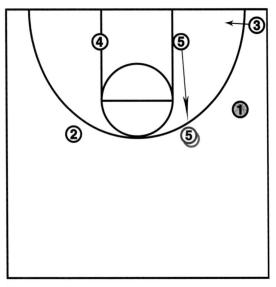

Diagram 4.10

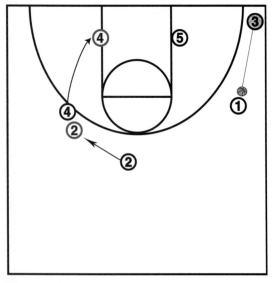

Diagram 4.9

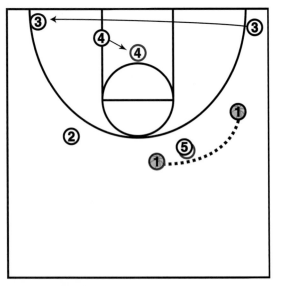

Diagram 4.11

Special Plays from Your Basic Zone Set

Scouting makes it very difficult to stay in one zone set. You should have two or three zone offenses or special plays off your basic set.

Lob Play to 3

This is a very familiar play where your posts will screen for the lob from 1 to 3. Start by passing around to 3 (Diagrams 4.12–4.14).

- 3 now passes back to 2, who swings to 1.
- On 3's pass to 2, 4 steps up to screen the center defending the zone while 5 comes across to back-screen the back forward who was guarding 3.

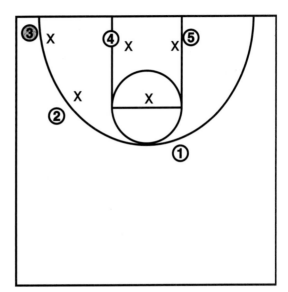

Diagram 4.13

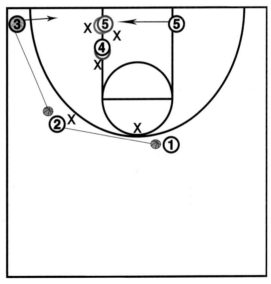

Diagram 4.14

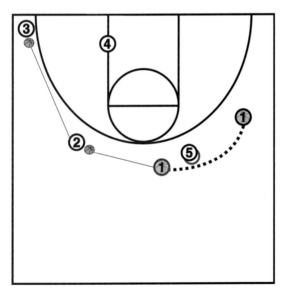

Diagram 4.12

These screens set the space needed for 3 to catch and dunk on the pass from 1 (Diagrams 4.15 and 4.16).

Should the lob not be there, 3 continues across and you're in your regular continuity (Diagram 4.17).

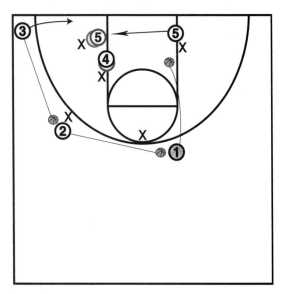

Diagram 4.15

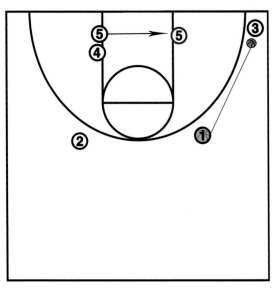

Diagram 4.17

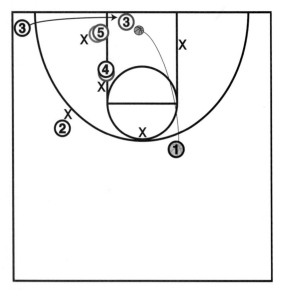

Diagram 4.16

Post Flash Play

- 2 stays ball side and slides down.
- 5 comes up and screens for 1.

On this screen, 4 flashes across to ball side block looking for a pass from 1 (Diagrams 4.18 and 4.19).

Again, if the pass is not there, 1 can pass to 2 and 2 can pass back to 1, 4 slides back, and 5 sets a screen for 1. 3 slides up and 2 becomes your corner runner, and you're in your continuity (Diagram 4.20).

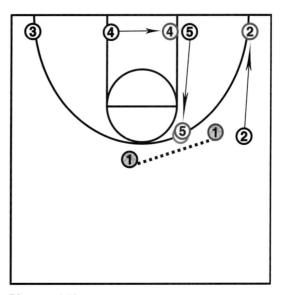

Diagram 4.19

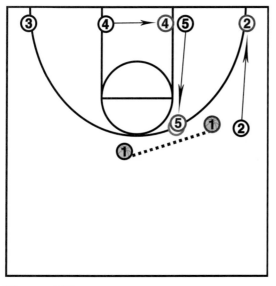

Diagram 4.18

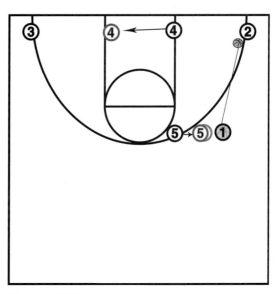

Diagram 4.20

Post Cross Screen

- 1 hits 2.
- 5 screens across for 4.
- 4 goes low and 5 comes back hard to the ball.

2 is looking to pass low to 4 or 5 to high. Should 5 receive the pass, he looks low to 4 or skip-passes to 3 (Diagrams 4.21–4.25).

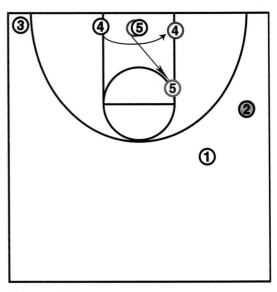

Diagram 4.22

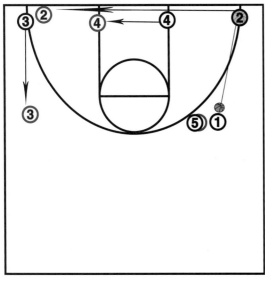

Diagram 4.21

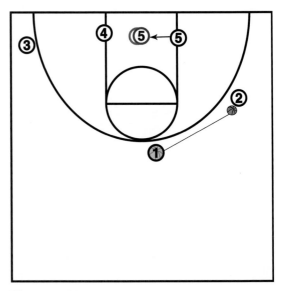

Diagram 4.23

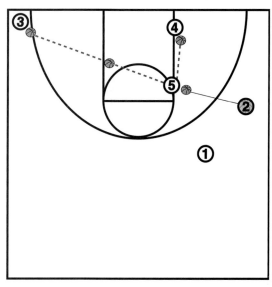

Diagram 4.24

Simple Post High-Low Attack

Against the 2-3 zone, many teams (including mine) will simply use a high-low post attack with three perimeter players freelancing outside (Diagram 4.26).

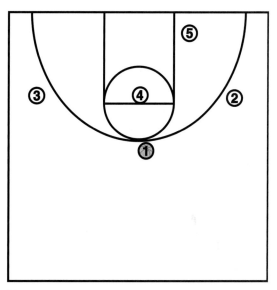

Diagram 4.26

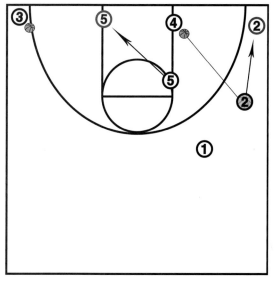

Diagram 4.25

- 1 hits 2.
- 5 posts up or can step out to the short corner.
- 4 flashes to the ball side elbow.
- 1 can hold or cut through and let 3 replace him (Diagrams 4.27 and 4.28).

- Should 2 hit 5, 4 immediately slides low.
- 2 spots up or slides low.
- 1 spots up and slides over, and 3 slides up (Diagrams 4.29 and 4.30).

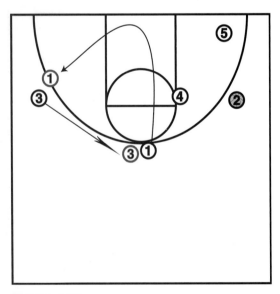

Diagram 4.27

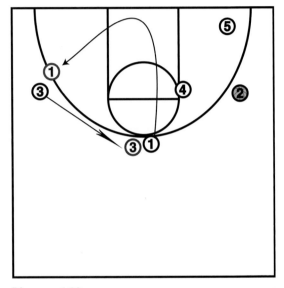

Diagram 4.29

Diagram 4.28

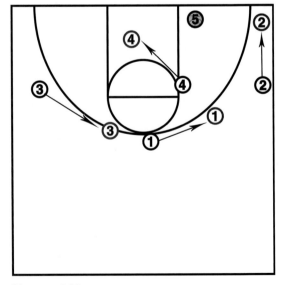

Diagram 4.30

Should 2 hit 4 at high post, 5 ducks in while 1, 2, and 3 spot up to open areas (Diagrams 4.31 and 4.32).

On the swing pass, the high post slides across and low while the low post slides up. This is called an "X" move (Diagrams 4.33 and 4.34).

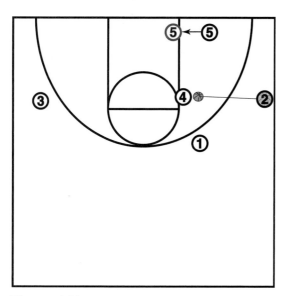

Diagram 4.31

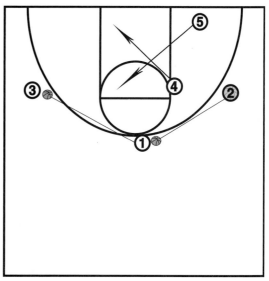

Diagram 4.33

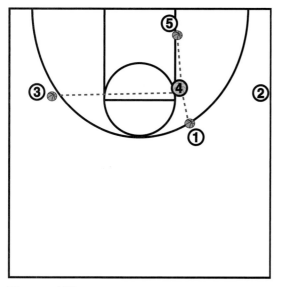

Diagram 4.32

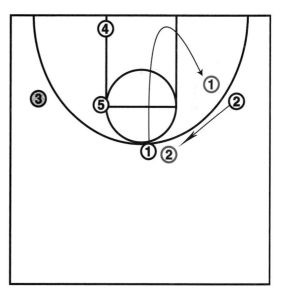

Diagram 4.34

VERSUS 3-2 ZONE

Middle or Corners Attack

An effective attack versus the 3-2 is to attack middle or corners.

- 1 passes to 2 and cuts behind 4, flashing high.
- 1 now goes to the ball side corner rather than the weak side.
- 3 holds on the weak side wing (Diagram 4.35).
- 2 looks low and high and then to 1 in the corner (Diagram 4.36).

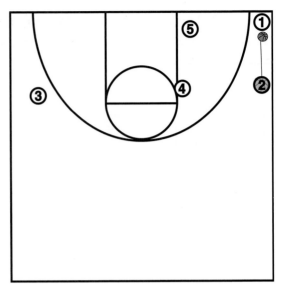

Diagram 4.36

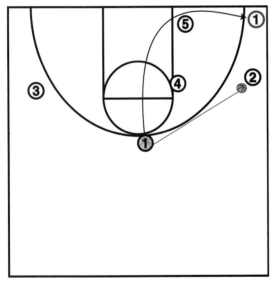

Diagram 4.35

- 2 then saddle-dribbles to the middle (Diagram 4.37).
- The posts (4 and 5) execute an "X" move, and 1 slides up.

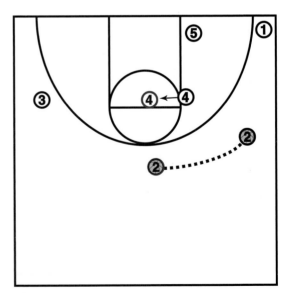

Diagram 4.37

- On the swing pass to 3, 2 cuts through the middle behind the post (5), flashing to the high post (Diagram 4.38).
- 2 cuts through to the ball side (Diagram 4.39).

At any time, your high post can step out to screen on the ball or step out to catch the ball.

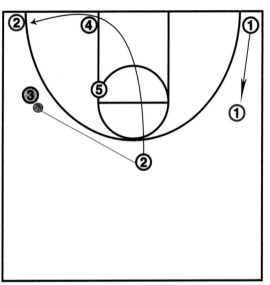

Diagram 4.39

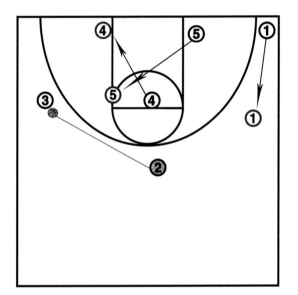

Diagram 4.38

VERSUS 1-3-1

2-1-2

We like to go to our 2-1-2 look versus the 1-3-1 zone (Diagram 4.40).

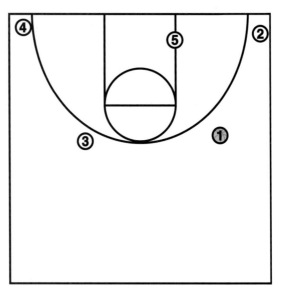

Diagram 4.41

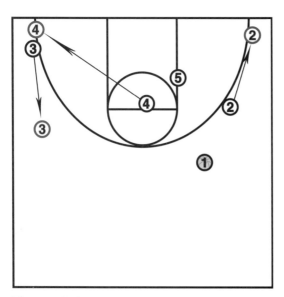

Diagram 4.40

2 slides down, 3 slides up, 4 goes to the opposite corner, and 5 works the middle (Diagram 4.41). On any pass to the corner, the corner player must be able to throw a diagonal skip pass to his teammate (Diagrams 4.42 and 4.43).

Make sure you also practice versus half-court zone traps, particularly the 1-3-1. Many teams will automatically trap corners, so make sure you have your outlets. When teams play a box-and-one defense, we use our zone or man attack. But again, it's important you practice against it so it doesn't disrupt your offensive flow.

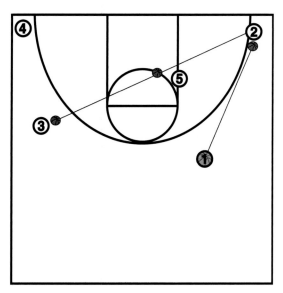

Diagram 4.42

Hopefully these various zone attacks can give you something to think about before you decide which zone offense to run. Again, the key is to keep that offense free-flowing and staying on the attack.

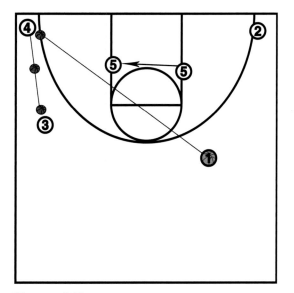

Diagram 4.43

CHAPTER 5

Special Situations

The best way to see how so many special situations can come about is to play some five-minute overtime games or even two- and one-minute games. These games must be played under game conditions. You will have to determine how many time-outs are left and the number of team fouls for each team. To practice coming from behind, just put one team ahead and get after them with your defensive pressure. Conversely, to work on protecting your lead and closing the deal, put one team ahead and work on your delay game. By doing these games, situations you never thought of will occur. These late-game situations will make or break your season, so practicing them is of utmost importance. Before you can get into these situational games, you need to have some things in place:

A. All out-of-bound plays, offensively and defensively
B. Last-second shots, including clock-going-down plays, and special
3-point-shot plays, should you need a 3. Out-of-bound plays, must also be done defensively
C. Free throw alignments, offensively and defensively
D. Pressure defense to make that comeback when behind, and your delay game to protect your lead and close the deal

Another situation that comes up a lot is to foul or not when you're up by 3 points and have very little time left. Dick Vitale says you should foul, but you had better practice and not commit a flagrant foul. Doing these special situations takes time, so you need to get your system in early to allow your team to practice these situations. There are so many inbound plays to learn from. Every game I watch I look for new ones. Any coach who is willing to learn can pick up great inbound plays from books, tapes, and clinics.

UNDER-THE-BASKET INBOUND PLAYS

We will use the 1-4 spread set. Another favorite set is the box set (Diagrams 5.1–5.3).

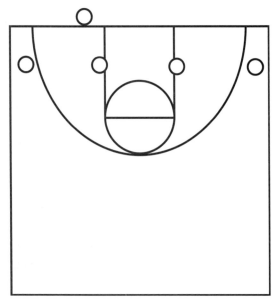

Diagram 5.1 Spread Set

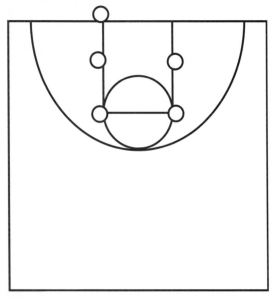

Diagram 5.2 Box Set

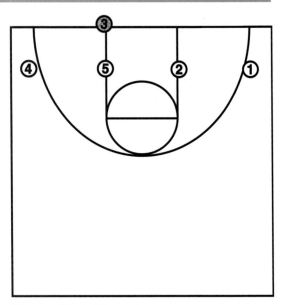

Diagram 5.3 1–4 Spread

1-4 Set, Screen the Screener

This is a common play that is very effective. 2 is your best shooter, 3 your best inbounder, 5 your center, 4 your strong forward, and 1 your safety man (Diagrams 5.4 and 5.5).

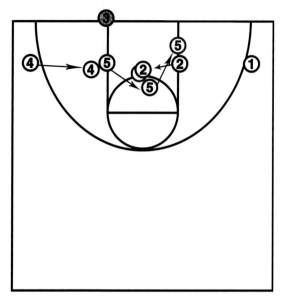

Diagram 5.4

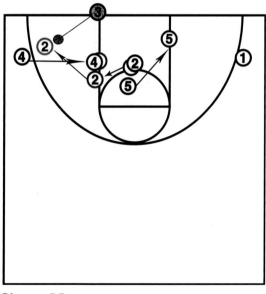

Diagram 5.5

- 5 steps up the lane and curls off 2's screen, looking for the lob pass.
- 4 comes to the lane and screens the screener (2) for the open shot.
- 3 also keeps an eye on 1 for a baseline pass.

Flex Option

If a pass from 3 to 2 is denied, 3 looks to 4. 3 can throw to 4 over the top and you can run the flex play from there.

- 4 catches the pass from 3 (Diagram 5.6).
- 5 comes high for pass from 4 (Diagram 5.7).
- 3 steps in and 2 can use 3's back screen, whereas 3 comes off 4's down screen (Diagram 5.8).

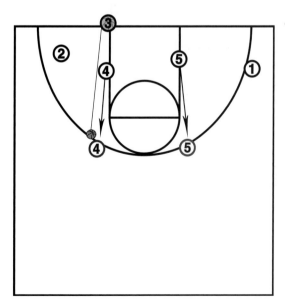

Diagram 5.6

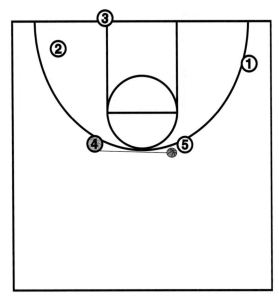

Diagram 5.7

2 Option

2 can fake using 3's screen and come off 4's down screen (Diagrams 5.9 and 5.10).

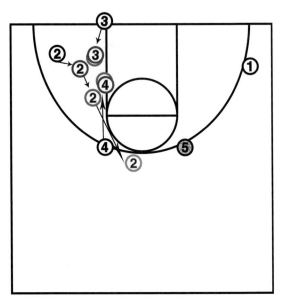

Diagram 5.9

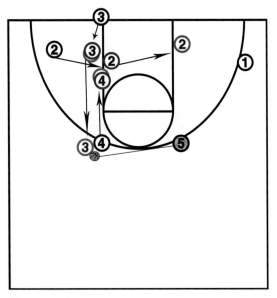

Diagram 5.8

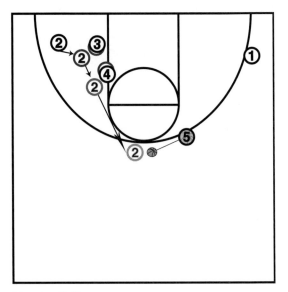

Diagram 5.10

Straight Flex

We sometimes run our flex play off our original 1-4 set.

- 3 throws over the top to 5. 2 comes up to receive the pass from 5 (Diagram 5.11).
- 3 steps in for a back screen. 4 uses 3's back screen, looking for a pass from 2 (Diagram 5.12).
- 3 then comes off 5's down screen for a pass from 2 (Diagram 5.13).

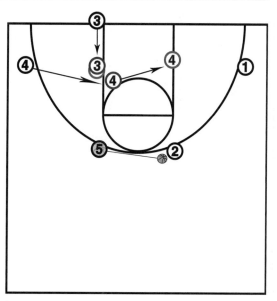

Diagram 5.12

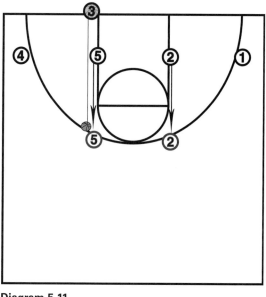

Diagram 5.11

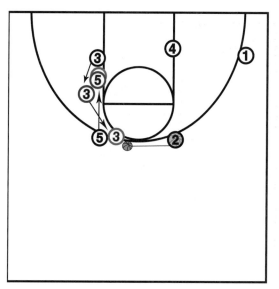

Diagram 5.13

Post Pop Out

Another play off this look is for 3 to pass to 4 (Diagram 5.14).

- 5 comes high and screens across for 2, who also came high (Diagram 5.15).
- 3 steps in to block and, on a 4 to 2 pass, 1 goes under the rim and will use a double screen set by 4 and 3 or a single screen set by 5 (Diagrams 5.16 and 5.17).

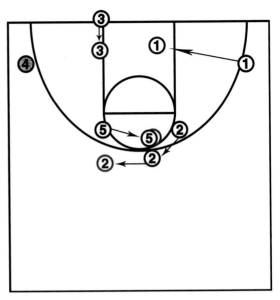

Diagram 5.15

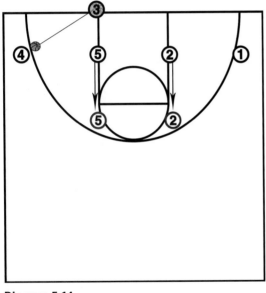

Diagram 5.14

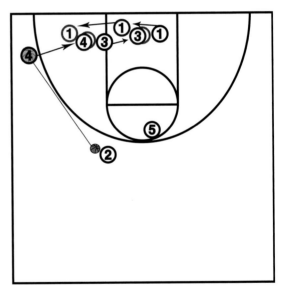

Diagram 5.16

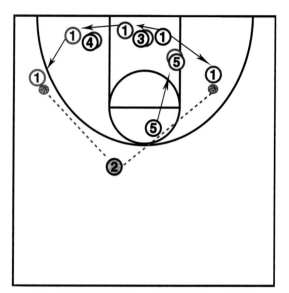

Diagram 5.17

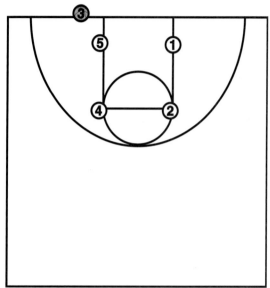

Diagram 5.18

Lob Play out of Box Set

Late in the game or shot clock, everybody needs a good lob play.

- 4 screens across for your best shooter 2 (Diagram 5.18). This is a decoy. While this is happening, 1 back-screens 5 for the lob dunk or a catch-and-shoot (Diagrams 5.19 and 5.20).

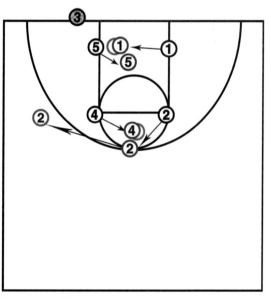

Diagram 5.19

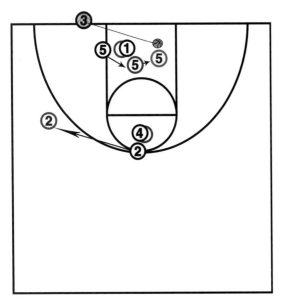

Diagram 5.20

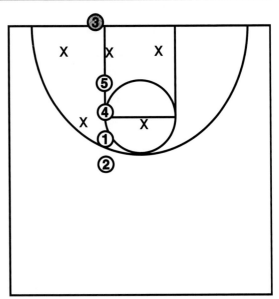

Diagram 5.21

Zone Inbound Play

So many coaches will ask me at clinics, "Coach, what if the defense is in a zone?" It's a good question, and keeping it in mind, you must have some zone inbound plays as well.

- 5 will bust to the rim (Diagram 5.21).
- 4 screens the top left wing while 1 screens the top right wing (Diagram 5.22).

- Hopefully, 2, your best shooter, will be open for a good 3-point shot (Diagram 5.23).

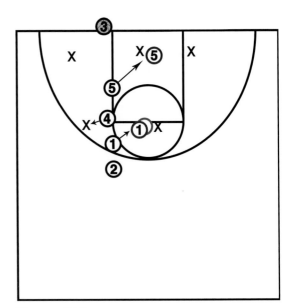

Diagram 5.22

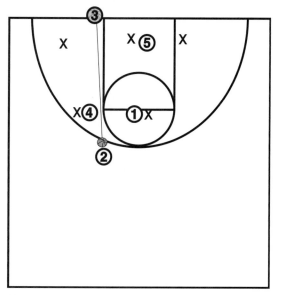

Diagram 5.23

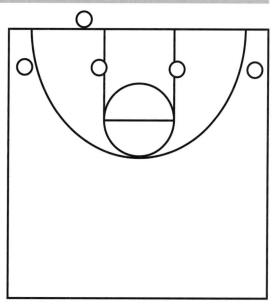

Diagram 5.24

SIDE INBOUND PLAYS

Side Inbound Short

Again, there are so many side inbound plays to learn from, and I always pick up one or two during the off-season. The line play is a very simple play where we put 4, 2, 1, and 5 in a straight line (Diagram 5.24).

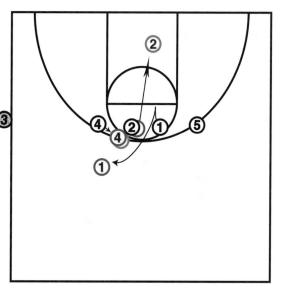

- 2 cuts to the rim while 4 screens for 1. 5 holds as an outlet (Diagram 5.25).
- 3 passes to 1 and immediately goes to block on his side (Diagram 5.26).
- 4 trails 3 and 5 screens down.
- 2 can use the double screen set by 3 and 4 or the single down screen by 5 (Diagram 5.27).

Diagram 5.25

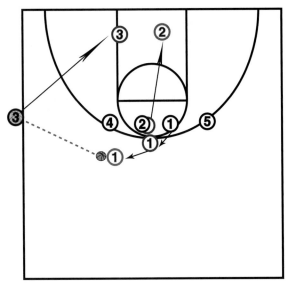

Diagram 5.26

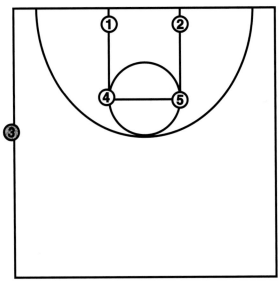

Diagram 5.28

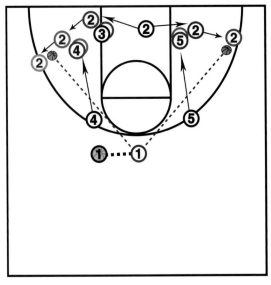

Diagram 5.27

Side Inbound Box Set

A very popular side inbound is off a box set.

- 1 slices off 4 for a 3 to 1 pass (Diagram 5.29).
- On the 3 to 1 pass, 5 pins down for 2 while 3, the inbounder, runs off staggered screens by 4 and 5 (Diagram 5.30).

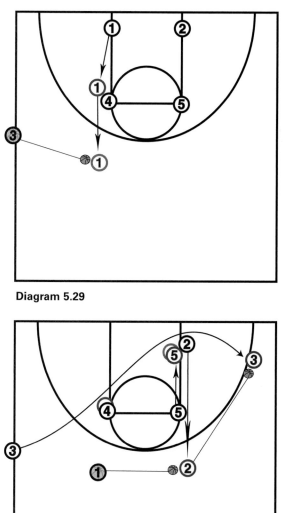

Diagram 5.29

On a 1 to 2 pass, rather than setting a low screen, 4 can stay high and set a flare screen for 1 (Diagrams 5.31 and 5.32).

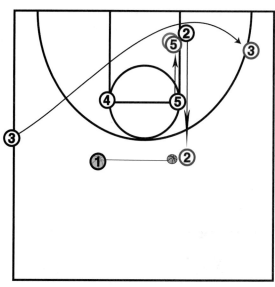

Diagram 5.31

Diagram 5.30

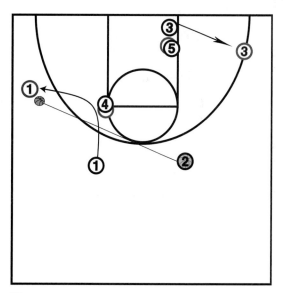

Diagram 5.32

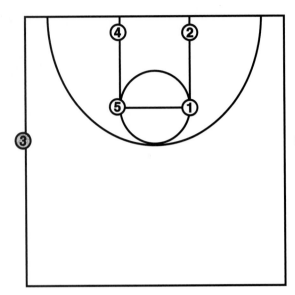

Diagram 5.33

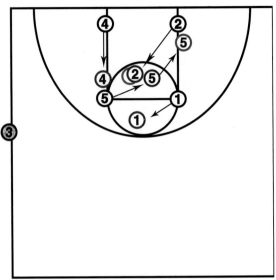

Diagram 5.34

Side Lob, Wrap Play

We still run this out of our box set but now put both posts on the ball side, and both 2 and 1 on the weak side (Diagram 5.33).

- 2 back-screens 5 for the lob (Diagram 5.34).
- 4 comes up to screen for 1, who wraps around 4 (Diagram 5.35).
- After the 1 to 4 wrap, 2 uses 4 and comes off looking for the open shot. After the 2 wrap, 4 pops out for a last option. 1 uses 5's screen for a 4 to 1 pass, if time allows (Diagram 5.36).

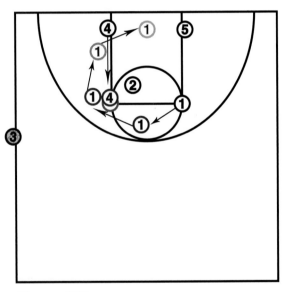

Diagram 5.35

Should the defense be in a zone, we usually try a lob play or a guard-through play.

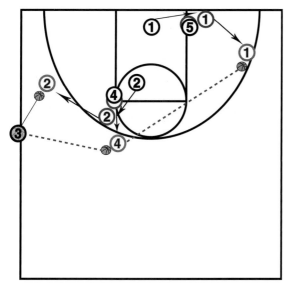

Diagram 5.36

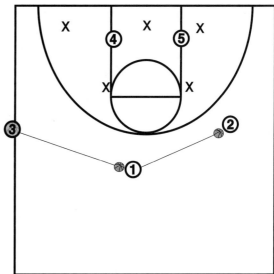

Diagram 5.37

Side Zone Lob Inbound

- 3 inbounds to 1, who swings to 2
  (Diagram 5.37).
- 3 runs the baseline, while 4 screens the
  defensive center and 5 back-screens 4.
- 2 looks for a lob to 3. If the lob is not
  there, 3 continues to the corner
  (Diagram 5.38).

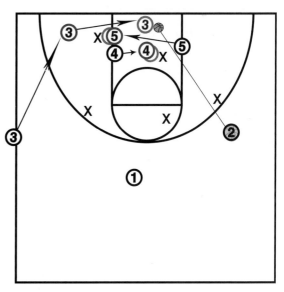

Diagram 5.38

Side Inbound Versus Zone

We call this a "through" play.

- 3 inbounds to 1, who swings to 2 (Diagram 5.39).
- 2 looks inside and goes back to 1, who goes back to 3 (Diagram 5.40).
- On the 1 to 3 pass, 2 goes to the middle of the foul line. 4 steps out high and wide.
- 3 passes back to 1, and then 4 and 3 build a wall for 2 to slide through for the shot (Diagram 5.41).

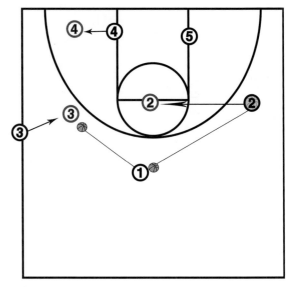

Diagram 5.40

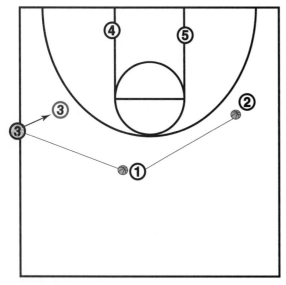

Diagram 5.39

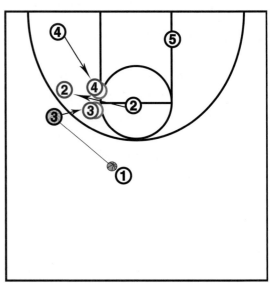

Diagram 5.41

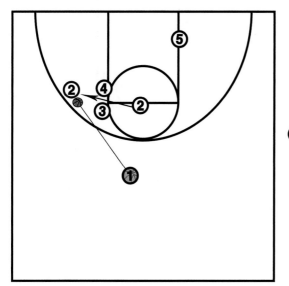

Diagram 5.42

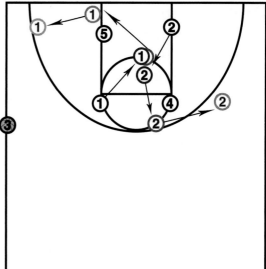

Diagram 5.43

Georgia Play for 3-Point Shot

We scrimmaged Georgia and they ran this against us, so we called it "Georgia."

From the box set:

- 1 down-screens for 2 and 2 fades off 4 (Diagram 5.42).
- 1 then curls around 5 back to the ball side (Diagram 5.43).
- 3 looks at 1 and then throws skip pass to 2 coming off 4's flair screen (Diagram 5.44)

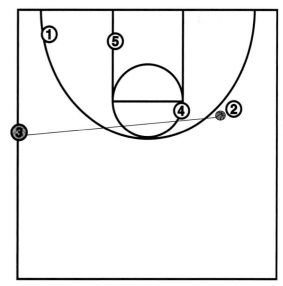

Diagram 5.44

Under Long Inbound Home Run

Everybody has an under home run play. I can think of two famous plays that are still talked about and worthy of any coach's playbook: one from Duke and another from Valparaiso University.

Duke

This is Grant Hill's perfect pass to Christian Laettner for the game-winning shot against Kentucky in 1992.

- 5 and 2 crisscross off 4 (Diagram 5.45).
- After the crisscross, 4 turns to catch the long pass from 3. It's a catch-and-shoot.

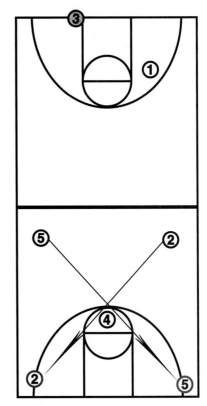

Diagram 5.45

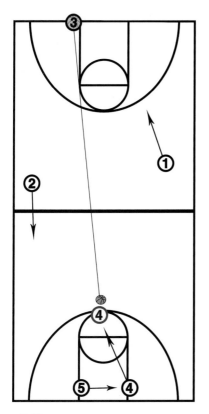

Diagram 5.46

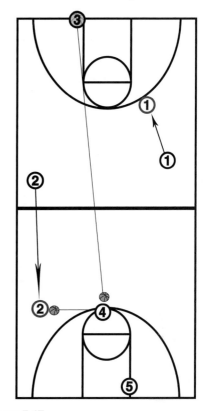

Diagram 5.47

Valparaiso

Coach Homer Drew had a little more time and ran a football play called "hook and ladder." Similar to Duke, a long pass was made, followed by an in-the-air catch and pass to Homer's son, Bryce, who caught the second pass and hit the game-winning shot (Diagrams 5.46 and 5.47).

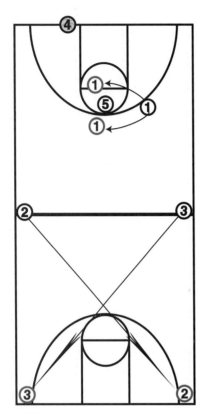

Diagram 5.48

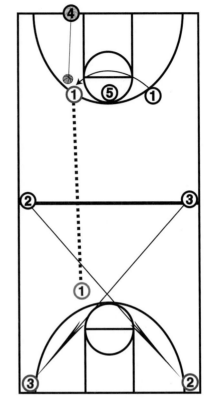

Diagram 5.49

Point Guard Play

I think these two famous plays give you a lot to think about and sets to work from. If there are at least five seconds left, we'll run a play where we try and get it to our point guard and let him speed-dribble to make a play.

- 1 uses 5 to get open.
- 3 and 2 cross over to the corners.
- 1 catches and speed-dribbles to make a play.

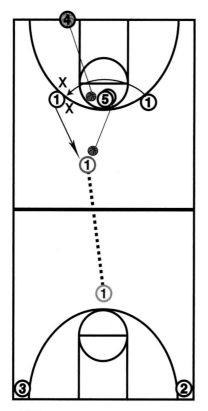

Diagram 5.50

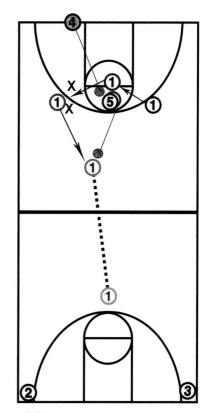

Diagram 5.51

Sometimes if 1 is double-teamed, you can throw to 5, who immediately passses to 1 on the run.

SIDE LONG INBOUND

We can run our same side short inbound play.

Box Lob and Wrap Play

- 2 will set a back screen for 5 while 1 wraps around 4.
- 2 then wraps around 4 to the ball side corner.
- 4 pops back to the ball (Diagrams 5.52 and 5.53).

Again, by doing certain minute games, all these situations will occur and you can see how

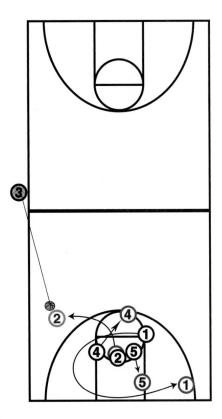

Diagram 5.53

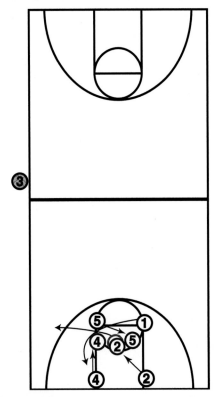

Diagram 5.52

important these plays are. If time allows, in under long home run situations you can pass to half-court and call a time-out. What's important is to get your team a makeable shot. To do this, you have to inbound the ball properly and, once inbounded, have scoring options.

DEFENDING INBOUND PLAYS

I love watching Syracuse University play so I can see how many teams score from out of bounds under and side versus their 2-3 zone.

Coach Boeheim loves his 2-3 zone and works hard during practice defending out-of-bound plays. Some teams start in zone and go man on the first pass. Others play straight-up man and may do some switching on screens. Gary Williams does his diamond trap defending all side out-of-bound plays. Dean Smith would take the defender on the ball, make him a basket protector, and deny all inbound passes from the side. Once the ball was inbounded, they usually went to their famous run-and-jump where they would double and trap the ball. It's your choice, so pick one and put it in.

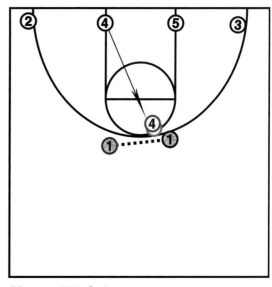

Diagram 5.54 Option 1

CLOCK-GOING-DOWN, LAST-SECOND SHOTS

Many teams use the high screen on the ball with the clock going down. So do we (Diagrams 5.54 and 5.55).

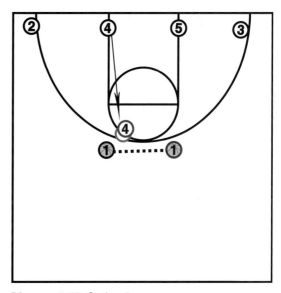

Diagram 5.55 Option 2

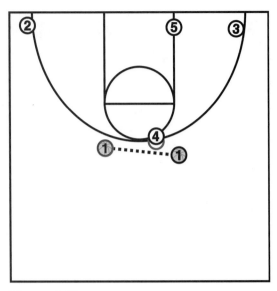

Diagram 5.56

However, teams will vary whether to spot up the post screener or roll him to the basket and replace him with the lost post. A lot depends on how your posts can shoot the ball. 4 screens and goes to best scoring area (Diagram 5.57).

Spot Up

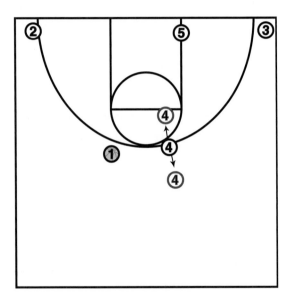

Diagram 5.57 4 Spots Up

We also will use an open look if you have a great penetrating point guard who can also make a pull-up jump shot should the defense sag off (Diagrams 5.58–5.60).

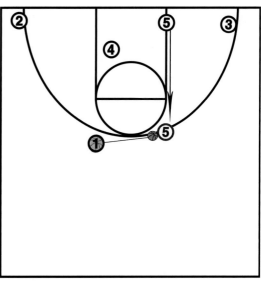

Diagram 5.59 5 Replaces

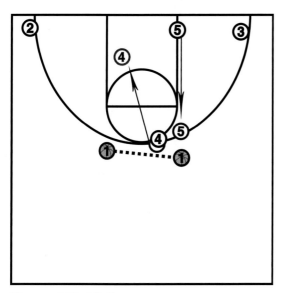

Diagram 5.58 4 Rolls

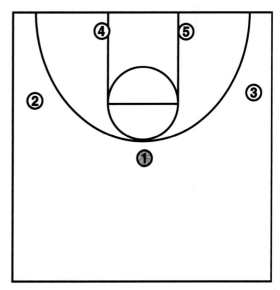

Diagram 5.60

Davidson

With the clock winding down, you can use some of your special plays whether it be a post isolation or staggered screen for a great shooter. Davidson College, a great team in our conference, loves to run a double high-post slip and screen that's really paid off for them with the clock going down. It's very tough to guard.

- 5 fakes a ball screen and slips to the basket (Diagram 5.61).
- 4 follows with a ball screen for 1 (Diagram 5.62).

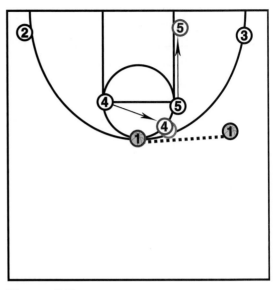

Diagram 5.62

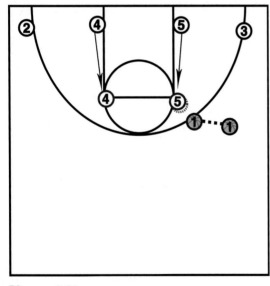

Diagram 5.61

Should you have a great shooter, just run him off some screens. Send him low to the middle of the rim and give him choices to go off a double or single (Diagrams 5.63 and 5.64).

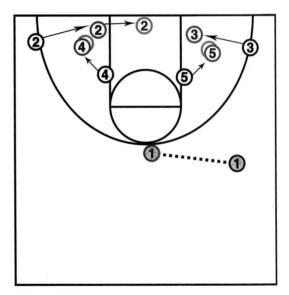

Diagram 5.63

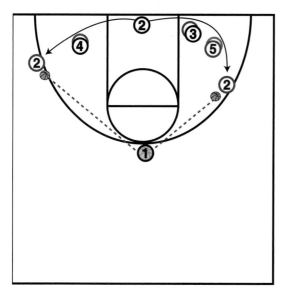

Diagram 5.64

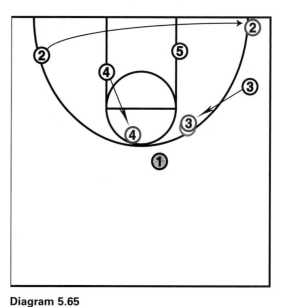

Diagram 5.65

3-POINT PLAYS

You always need some good 3-point plays when you're down 3 and need a 3-ball.

- 3 comes up and screens for 1.
- 2 (the weak side wing) goes to the ball side off 5 (Diagram 5.65).
- 3 then uses 4's flare screen for the 3-point shot (Diagram 5.66).

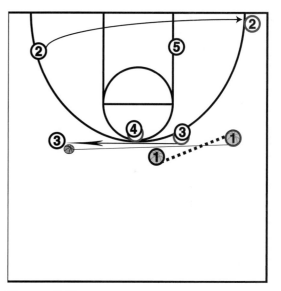

Diagram 5.66

If 2 is your best shooter, 1 can pass to 3, cut low, and set a triple staggered screen for 2. 3 becomes the point guard on this play (Diagrams 5.67 and 5.68)

FOUL-LINE ALIGNMENTS

A lot of things upset coaches, and missed-shot free throw rebounds by the offense are right up there. Conversely, the coach of the offensive team is delighted to get a second chance to score. You're allowed six players in the lanes plus the free throw shooter. The defense gets four on the line while the offense gets two plus the shooter (Diagram 5.69).

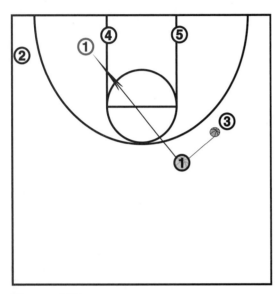

Diagram 5.67

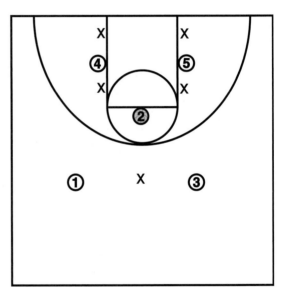

Diagram 5.69

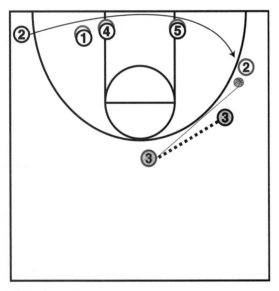

Diagram 5.68

Defense

- Both Xs on 4's side double-team 4 and block him out.
- X on 5's side has one-on-one block-out responsibility, while X above 5 will take the shooter, who can't leave until the ball hits the rim (Diagram 5.70).

All other players have to remain outside the 3-point arc.

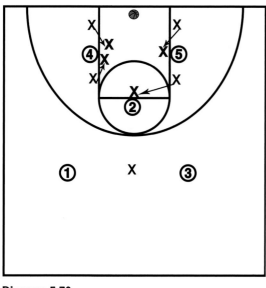

Diagram 5.70

Offense

- 4 and 5 communicate with each other and one of them will be the go guy. 4 tells 5, "I am going," and on the free throw shot will go hard at the X on 5's side. 5 cuts behind 4 to the rim looking for a rebound (Diagram 5.71).

It's like 4 is screening for 5. If 5 says he's the "go-to" man, he goes at the X on 4's side. 4 then cuts behind 5 to the rim looking for the offensive rebound.

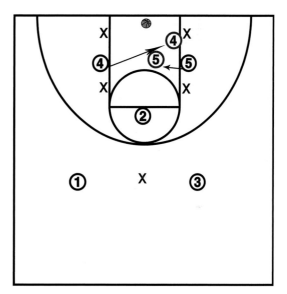

Diagram 5.71

DELAY GAME

Coaches love to protect leads and close the deal for the win. This is done by managing the clock and getting a good shot off before time expires. It's a great feeling to be up and score in your delay game as the clock is going down.

When I first arrived in the ACC in 1981, it was one year after Mike Krzyzewski went to Duke and Jim Valvano went to North Carolina State. Our target, along with everybody else, was the great Dean Smith and his North Carolina Tar Heels. Coach Smith made his delay game very famous. I played against Coach Smith's teams when I played for his and my mentor, Frank McGuire, at the University of South Carolina.

Coach Smith, without a shot clock and the 3-point shot, loved to go to his four corners delay game when his team took a lead. Phil Ford took the four corners to a new level with his incredible penetrating, ball handling, passing, and scoring ability. It was very difficult to guard because of great spacing. Today, even with the shot clock and 3-point shot, teams will go to a four corners spread (Diagram 5.72).

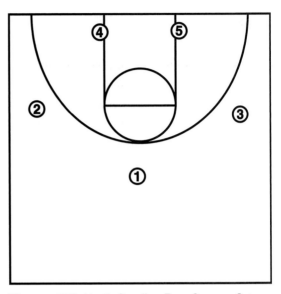

Diagram 5.72 North Carolina Four Corners Set

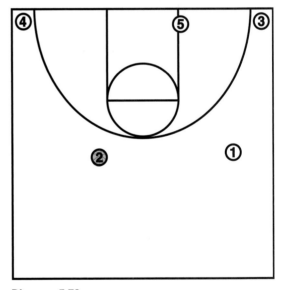

Diagram 5.73

North Carolina Four Corners Set

What I see a lot of today is 4-out or 5-out. With 4-out, the first inside player tries to stay opposite the ball (Diagram 5.73).

4-Out

The 4-out guys are passing, cutting and re-placing, penetrating, and keeping good floor balance with proper spacing. Having two big posts could force a big man outside handling the ball, so you must know what's best for your personnel. The great aspect about 4-out is the middle being wide open for either penetration and score or penetration and kick.

5-Out

Again, it's passing and cutting to the basket, but if you don't receive a pass you get out to the opposite corner, players rotate to open areas and keep that middle open (Diagram 5.74).

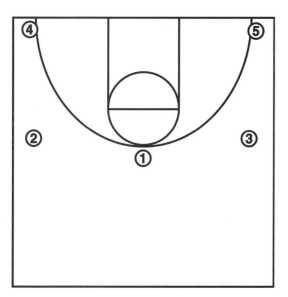

Diagram 5.74

Over the past couple of years I have been running our half-court offense without shooting unless it's a layup or wide-open shot. Once we reach the 10- to 8-second mark and we haven't taken our high-percentage shot, we'll run our clock-going-down shot.

I am actually studying our personnel as I write this book to see what our best delay game will be for next season. I am leaning toward trying the 4-out or 5-out spread.

You also need your delay game when there is a tie or a 1-point difference late in the game. I am not averse to holding the ball for the last shot down 1. It might be better to do on the road, but I'll do it at home also. All these situations will occur when you do those 7-, 5-, 3-, 2-, or 1-minute games. Obviously, you need to work on the defending team's delay games. The worst thing you can do is foul late in the clock and bail the offense out by letting them go to the free throw line or gaining a new shot clock. You may want to defend straight up or trap. No matter what, the key is to work on it.

USING THE 1-2-2 TO SPARK A COMEBACK

We'll play minute games where we're behind and need to go to full-court pressure and try to make a comeback. Coming from behind to win is a special feeling.

The past year, playing in the Puerto Rico Tip-Off against Temple University, we found ourselves down 25 at the half. Arkansas had beaten us by 30 in the first game. Walking to the locker room I was thinking of my close friends asking me, "Why did you ever go back to coaching?" I was biting my tongue to stay calm and confident. We had a 1-2-2 three-quarter press in our pressure scheme. I said, "Let's set a goal to be down 10 at the 10-minute mark. We'll go to our 1-2-2 and, most important, let's play the game, not the score." Little did I realize what was about to happen.

The 1-2-2 disrupted Temple and we got some steals and scores. After a couple of Temple turnovers, the trend continued, and, lo and behold, we started to get back in the game. I was feeling very proud just to get back in, but the comeback continued and Dustin Scott, our strong forward, made an incredible shot at the buzzer to give us the win. Temple's coach, Fran Dunphy, showed his class after the game. I felt bad for him, but all he said was "Congratulations." That was one of the greatest comebacks I have ever seen.

I appreciated Fran's words in a tough situation for him. Temple went on to get a win the next night and have a great second-half season, winning the Atlantic 10 championship

and an NCAA bid. I could never describe the feeling I had after that win—there just can't be a higher high. It's part of what coaching is all about. There was nothing special about our 1-2-2 three-quarter press. If you're a coach, you're very familiar with it.

- 3 usually traps with 1 or 2.
- The weak side guard (1 or 2) cheats to the middle.
- The ball side post (5 or 4) cheats to the sideline while the other post defends the rim (Diagrams 5.75 and 5.76).

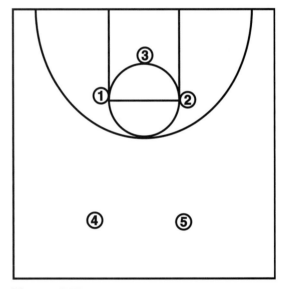

Diagram 5.75

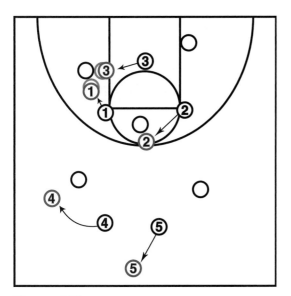

Diagram 5.76

Our 3 man was long and he forced deflections, which led to Temple's turnovers. After that Temple game, all our opponents worked versus the 1-2-2, so it wasn't as effective. That's when you need to adjust or maybe go to a man-to-man full-court pressure.

I think you're getting the gist of what I am talking about. It's somewhat about the scheme, but it's more about the heart of your team and that you have prepared them for all these possible situations.

CHAPTER 6

Point Guard Play

Looking back at my career, most of our teams' success can be attributed to the great point guards I was fortunate to coach. It all started in 1975 when, at the age of 27, I was hired at Appalachian State University (ASU) in Boone, North Carolina. The Southern Conference at the time had excellent teams including the University of Richmond, Furman University, Davidson College, Marshall University, and the Virginia Military Institute (VMI), who went to the Elite Eight in the 1976 NCAA Tournament under former NBA coach Bill Blair. I would like to share with you the characteristics of these great point guards and what I learned from them.

DARRYL ROBINSON

When I was hired by ASU, I immediately called Tom Kochanski, a New York basketball scout who now is Howie Garfinkel's Five-Star right-hand man. Tom is a good friend who directed me to Darryl Robinson, a 6-foot 3-inch guard out of South Shore High School in Brooklyn, New York. I found Darryl to be a

tall point guard who was very intelligent and, with his New York background, understood how to play the game. He was an excellent ball handler and, although not a great outside shooter, he could really drive to the basket. His height and intelligence made Darryl a very good defensive player. These attributes immediately attracted me to Darryl.

Sure enough, Darryl, with his smarts and his love of driving, led us in scoring most of his great career at ASU. His driving also got him to the foul line a lot where he was an excellent free throw shooter, especially in the clutch. He told me because of his height and smarts he wanted to guard the opposition's best perimeter player. That's exactly what I did when I played for the late Hall of Famer Frank McGuire, so you know I loved that. I also knew I had a leader with heart. That's a coach's dream.

It was an easy decision to put the ball in Darryl's hands and let him be our leader. Coaches need to figure out whose hands they want the ball in. That person will be your leader. We loved to set ball screens for Darryl because of his smarts. He would drag (be patient) with the ball screen, and it would open up a lot of scoring opportunities for Darryl and his teammates.

On this play, Darryl used the high screen set by 4. Darryl could shoot, drive, or pass. The high screener (4) rolled and the low post (5) replaced the high post. The wings (3 and 2) stayed deep in the corner ready to shoot should their defenders try to help on Darryl. It was a perfect play for Darryl and his teammates (Diagrams 6.1–6.4).

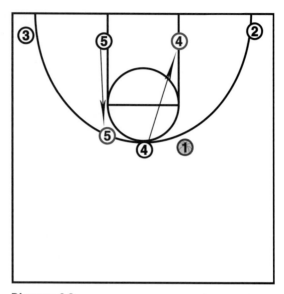

Diagram 6.2

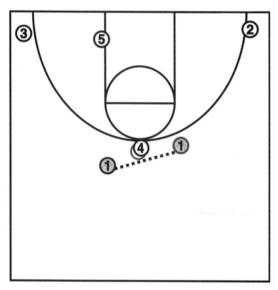

Diagram 6.1

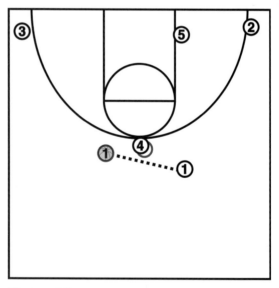

Diagram 6.3

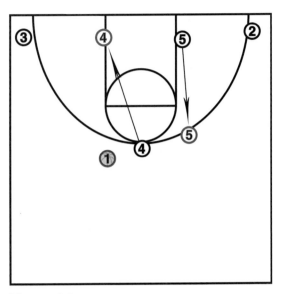

Diagram 6.4

In 1978 Darryl and his teammates gained ASU new respect with its first NCAA bid, and we were on our way. Darryl, with great leadership, ball handling, scoring, and defense, was the tournament's Most Valuable Player. He ranks third all-time in ASU history for field goals made.

While out of coaching, as a TV analyst I had the pleasure of doing some Clemson University games where Darryl's son, Shawan, played. Shawan was a star on and off the court and gave so much credit to his dad, who coached him at Leesville Road High School in Raleigh, North Carolina. Darryl now coaches at Hillside High School in Durham. The day I recruited Darryl was a very special day in my early career. He brought along another New Yorker named Mel Hubbard who could really jump and block shots. Darryl and Mel gave us a great foundation on which to build a program.

WALTER ANDERSON

After Darryl graduated, we recruited a different type of point guard, Walter Anderson from New Hanover High School in Wilmington, North Carolina, home of Michael Jordan. Walter was small at 5 feet 11 inches, but very, very quick. He couldn't see the court like Darryl, but his quickness and powerful build made Walter very hard to defend. He could really handle the ball by keeping it very low to the ground and had a great crossover move that was a killer. Because of Walter's quickness and strength, we decided to recruit him. Sure enough, no one in the conference could guard him. He would blow by defenders and score.

Where Darryl loved the high ball screen, Walter loved open space. We, therefore, used a 1-4 look for Walter that was very effective (Diagrams 6.5 and 6.6).

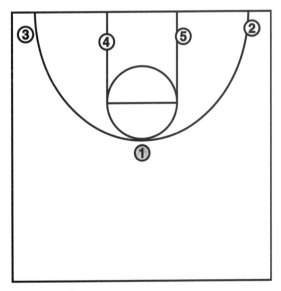

Diagram 6.5

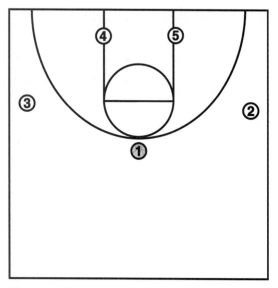

Diagram 6.6

Coaches need to figure out what plays work best for their personnel, especially when the shot clock is going down and on last second shots. It can win you a lot of games in late-game situations.

A good anecdote regarding Walter involved my assistant Kevin Cantwell, who I sent to scout a Citadel vs. University of North Carolina Wilmington (UNCW) game. Kevin called me to tell me he had made a mistake about the location of the game. Instead of being at Wilmington, the game was actually being held at the Citadel. Since he was already in Wilmington, Kevin instead went to a high school game and saw Walter play and loved his quickness. Walter was stubborn. I once sent a sub in for Walter. The sub came back to the bench and told me Walter refused to come out. It was a good test for a young coach, but

I didn't hesitate to suspend him after the game. Walter eventually came back to the team and led us to some very good wins.

MARK PRICE

In 1981, after six years at ASU, I went to Georgia Tech (GT). I'll always remember my first staff meeting with my assistants: George Felton, a former South Carolina head coach, a onetime assistant under Tubby Smith at Kentucky, and now the director of college scouting for the San Antonio Spurs; and Ben Jobe, a former NBA assistant and head coach at Southern University. I told George and Ben we needed to make recruiting a point guard a top priority. I had seen what Darryl and Walter did for our program at ASU and I felt the right point guard could possibly do the same for us at Georgia Tech. I told my staff I knew it would be hard to recruit a great center, but there were lots of point guards out there. A few weeks later, I received a call from George, who told me he had found the guy we needed in Jacksonville, Florida. Atlanta is not too far from Jacksonville and I knew we had a strong GT Club in Jacksonville. However, after George told me that he was at a summer Amateur Athletic Union tournament and this young man was from Enid, Oklahoma, I got totally depressed. I yelled at George over the phone, "How the hell are we going to get a kid out of Enid, Oklahoma?" I had never taken a step in the state of Oklahoma and had no idea where the heck Enid was.

Courtesy of Georgia Tech Athletic Association.

Mark Price

shooting range and he was definitely quick enough. I felt he could learn to be a playmaker to go along with his scoring. I also felt Mark could be our foundation at the point, and thus began a long and enjoyable courtship of the very spiritual and singing Price family.

Along with his talent, Mark had tremendous character and faith. He was a born-again Christian whose faith meant everything to him. When he had visited Oral Roberts University, Dr. Roberts took him alone to the school's chapel and told Mark he had a vision the previous night where God had told him Mark should go to his school. Now, that's recruiting pressure.

Mark was also an excellent student and represented what I called "the total package." However, because of his size there were many doubters, so I had some concern if Mark could actually play in the tough ACC.

George and I had to camp out in the Enid Holiday Inn for a week before Mark finally called my room and said he was coming. Luck plays an important role in recruiting. Mark indeed wanted to play in the ACC but favored North Carolina. Fortunately for us, UNC signed another point guard, also from Oklahoma, by the name of Steve Hale. That upset Mark and he was determined to prove his critics wrong. It didn't take long to see we did indeed have a special player. With Mark we brought along a skinny 6-foot 11-inch New Yorker named John "Spider" Salley and a junior college transfer named Yvon Joseph, a 6-foot 11-inch bruiser from Haiti.

George convinced me to go to Enid and watch Mark Price play. My first impression of Mark showed me a small, 6-foot scoring guard who was quick and had lots of heart. Mark's late dad, Denny Price, was an assistant under John MacLeod at both Oklahoma University and with the Phoenix Suns, so I knew Mark knew how to play. I couldn't get over his

John and Yvon gave us inside presence to go along with Mark's perimeter play. During Mark's freshman year, the ACC experimented with the 3-point line and it played perfectly into Mark's game and made him an even more exciting player.

We ran a lot of plays for Mark, some with the ball in his hands, others with him off the ball using screens. With the ball, we ran both of the previous plays I showed you for Darryl and Walter. Mark was excellent at both, so we mixed them up (Diagrams 6.7 and 6.8).

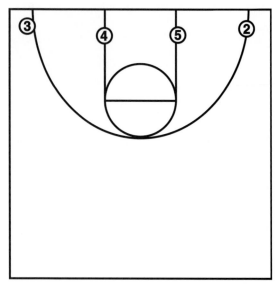

Diagram 6.8

Off the ball, we ran a lot of UCLA post cuts for Mark where he would use the back screen and cut or fake using it and pop back for the pass (Diagrams 6.9 and 6.10).

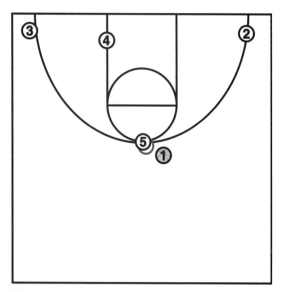

Diagram 6.7

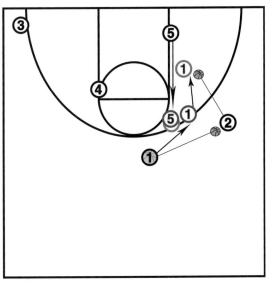

Diagram 6.9

When he used the back screen, he would then use 2's screen when 2 reversed the ball to 5 (Diagrams 6.11 and 6.12).

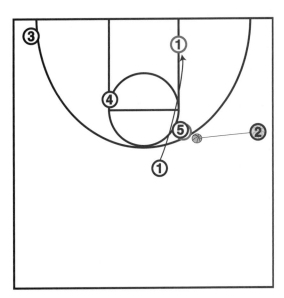

Diagram 6.11

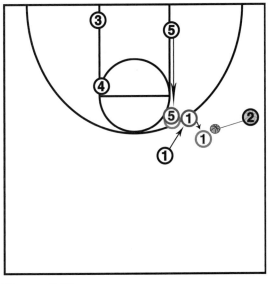

Diagram 6.10

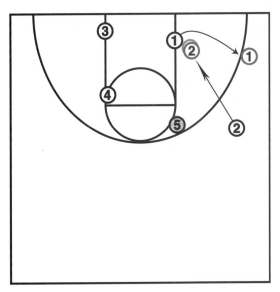

Diagram 6.12

5 would look for 1 (Mark), or when 5 would reverse the ball to 3, he would set another screen for 1 (Mark) (Diagrams 6.13 and 6.14).

Sometimes Mark would pass the ball to the wing or go low to use a single or double screen (Diagram 6.15).

Here, 2 dribbles to the middle and replaces 1 as point guard. Again, 1 can use either the double set by 3 and 4 or the single set by 5 (Diagrams 6.16 and 6.17).

We also loved to set post trail screens for Mark on our fast break. Being a great shooter, Mark only needed a little space to get open for the 3-point shot (Diagrams 6.18 and 6.19).

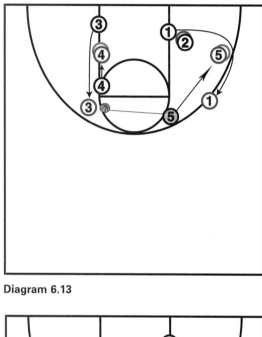

Diagram 6.13

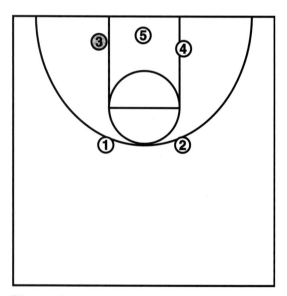

Diagram 6.15

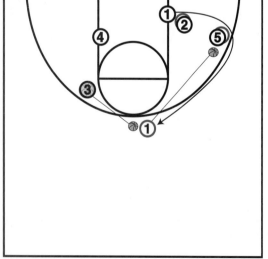

Diagram 6.14

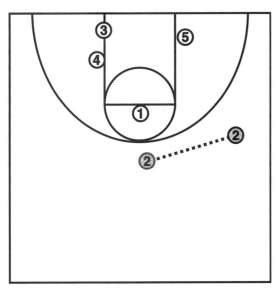

Diagram 6.16

With the transition defense protecting the inside, a post trail screen was very effective. It's even more effective when that post trail can screen, pop, and shoot (Diagrams 6.18 and 6.19).

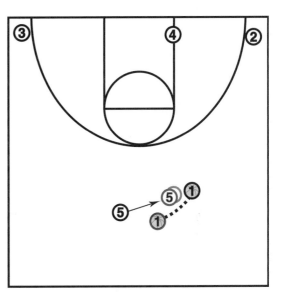

Diagram 6.18

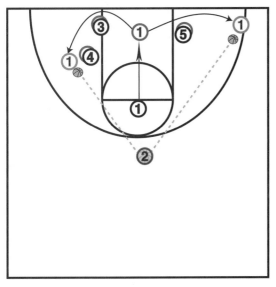

Diagram 6.17

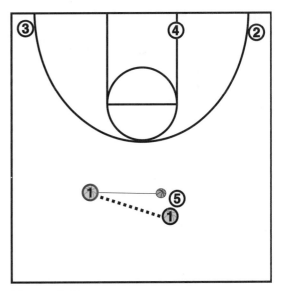

Diagram 6.19

Mark became the talk of the ACC and was named ACC Rookie of the Year. We had our foundation and now all we needed was to add a few more pieces. We were definitely on our way and the excitement for our program was growing, which really helped recruiting. The following year we signed our first McDonald's All-American, Bruce Dalrymple, a slashing, rebounding wing player. Mark, being very coachable and intelligent, and wanting his team to win, easily adjusted to being a pure point guard and not just a scorer.

Our shining moment came in the 1985 ACC Tournament in our hometown of Atlanta. After beating Virginia and Duke in the first and second round, we had to beat UNC and the incomparable Dean Smith for the third time after having swept them in the regular season. Of course, Mark made the winning free throws and was the tournament's Most Valuable Player. I regret we didn't get to the Final Four and make a national championship run with Mark and his teammates. In 1985, we came close but lost in an Elite Eight game to John Thompson's Georgetown University team with Patrick Ewing, and in 1986, we were upset in an Atlanta Sweet 16 by Dale Brown's Louisiana State University Tigers.

Besides being ACC Rookie of the Year in 1983, Mark was a three-time all-American, made first team in 1985, was a four-time All-ACC choice, and after being drafted by Dallas was traded to Cleveland. The Mark Price—Brad Daugherty pick-and-roll was a thing of beauty. Mark's jersey is retired at Georgia Tech and Cleveland. He's married to a GT girl named Laura, has four children, and lives in Atlanta, where we continue to have a fond relationship. Mark believed his coming to GT was a godsend, so I thanked God many times for sending Mark my way.

CRAIG NEAL

After Mark, we turned the ball over to Craig Neal, who had played two years with Mark. Craig's dad, Stan, coached him at Washington High School in Washington, Indiana. George Felton found Craig, and when I first saw Craig play, I saw a tall, skinny, play-all-out guard. I figured with his dad being a coach, Craig would learn to play at different speeds. At times, his all-out play was a problem because Craig would have some wild, ugly turnovers and my Irish temper would be tested, but Craig would come back and make an unbelievable play that brought the house down.

Craig Neal

Craig was good at getting us in our half-court sets, but his real strength was the open court. I once asked him why he loved to push the ball. Without hesitating he said, "Coach, it's the easiest way to score." Craig was injured his sophomore year and had to be red-shirted. This helped his maturity a lot, and when he was a senior he actually could play at two speeds.

For Craig to be effective, I had to give him freedom to create. He loved setting his teammates up and I loved that. Coaches never want to hold a player back, but the player must also earn that freedom by first playing defense and second being unselfish. Craig earned that freedom and it was fun to let him go.

Craig still holds Georgia Tech records for assists in a single game (19) and in a season (303 in 1988). He ranks 17th in ACC career assists and third all-time at GT. Craig, a former NBA assistant, is an associate head coach under Steve Alford, first at the University of Iowa and now at the University of New Mexico.

Brian Oliver

BRIAN OLIVER

I was also very fortunate to recruit a player who could play point or wing (combo guard) in Brian Oliver. I almost blew Brian's recruiting because I wasn't sure what position he played. Brian taught me the true value of a versatile player. Watching Brian do so many different things at times confused me. Brian's ability to play the 1, 2, or 3 gave us a diamond in the rough. I highly recommend recruiting a versatile player.

Having a versatile player like Brian can really protect your team from injuries and foul trouble. Grant Hill from Duke is one of the all-time great versatile players. Once, when we were playing Duke, Bobby Hurley, their outstanding point guard, was out with an injury. Coach K moved Grant to the point and they beat us without Bobby. Brian did that for us. I played Brian everywhere and we never lost a beat. We would put Brian at the point, run the UCLA post cut, and post him up (Diagrams 6.20 and 6.21).

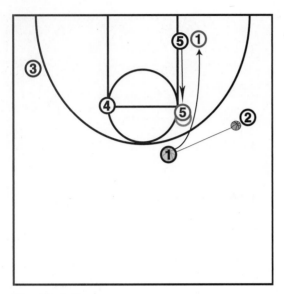

Diagram 6.20

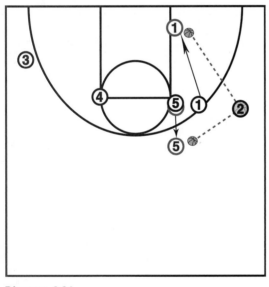

Diagram 6.21

2 could swing to 5, 5 could swing to 4, and 4 could swing to 3 while Brian continued to post up (Diagram 6.22).

Brian was an exceptional rebounder, and when we played him at the point and 2, I would worry about our transition defense. However, his rebounding instincts made me say the heck with it. Brian was also an exceptional person and student. He played briefly in the NBA, his versatility has allowed him to be an outstanding European player, and he just returned to Georgia Tech at the age of 39 to finish his degree.

Again, find a versatile player and it will help your team immediately. Brian's favorite line to me was, "Coach, I don't care where I play, just put me out there." Thank God I listened. Brian was Most Valuable Player in the 1990 ACC Tournament and with his two other Lethal Weapon buddies, Kenny Anderson and Dennis Scott, got us to the Final 4 in 1990. Brian

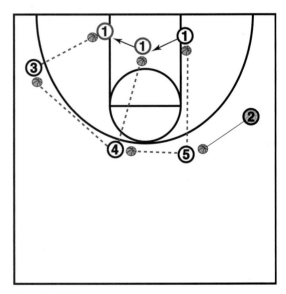

Diagram 6.22

was the only player in Tech history to accumulate more than 1,000 points, 500 rebounds, and 500 assists. Now, that's versatility.

DENNIS SCOTT

Dennis Scott at 6 feet 8 inches was not a point guard, but his point guard mentality made me change my fast-break philosophy. Dennis was recruited by my assistant, Perry Clark. Perry played at DeMatha Catholic High School for the famous Morgan Wootten and knew the Washington, D.C.–Virginia area very well. Perry went on to coach at Tulane University and the University of Miami and, after taking a turn as a TV analyst like me, is back coaching at Texas A&M, Corpus Christi.

Dennis, of course, is known as one of the best 3-point shooters ever in college basketball. He had very deep range but could also handle the rock and was a great passer. One day in practice he rebounded and waited for the point guard to come back to receive the pass from him. It delayed our break and, having learned what a great passer he was, I decided to let him lead the break when he rebounded the ball. He loved becoming the point guard and making all kinds of passes.

Dennis rebounds and immediately becomes the point guard. 1 must fill the ball

Dennis Scott

side lane, 2 fills the weak side, 4 goes to the middle, and 5 becomes the trail (Diagrams 6.23–6.26).

Dennis now has all the options of a point guard. He can drive and kick, pass and cut through, or use 5 (the post trail) as a screen (Diagrams 6.27–6.31).

One catch to this is teaching your 1 man to fill a lane. Kenny Anderson used to stand and watch Dennis go, but eventually he got the hang of it and actually liked being a wing and filling a lane for a drive or a pull-up jumper.

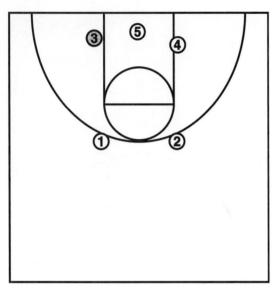

Diagram 6.23

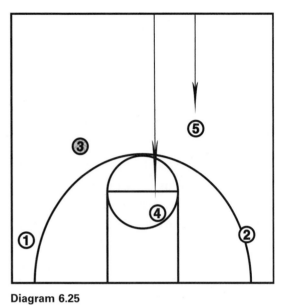

Diagram 6.25

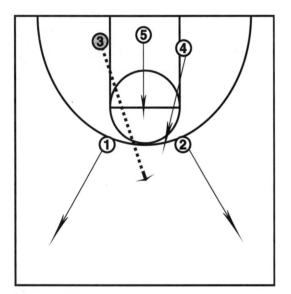

Diagram 6.24

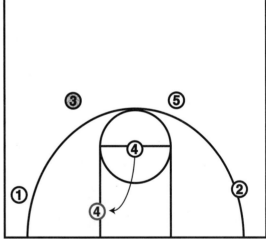

Diagram 6.26 Drive and Kick

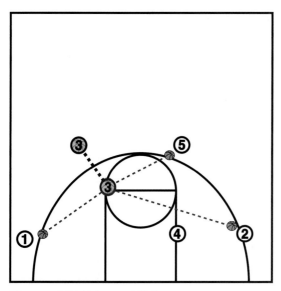

Diagram 6.27 Drive and Kick

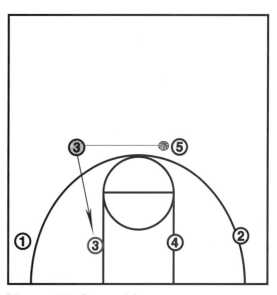

Diagram 6.29 Pass and Cut

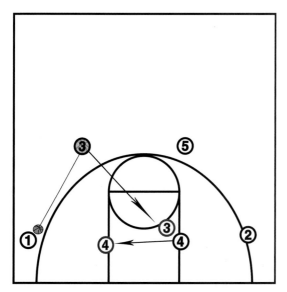

Diagram 6.28 Pass and Cut

Our break became faster, less predictable, and absolutely more fun. Should you have a player who has a point guard mentality, I recommend you try this. Now, if I were doing a book on shooting, there would be a whole chapter on Dennis, but I did enjoy watching him transform to a point guard.

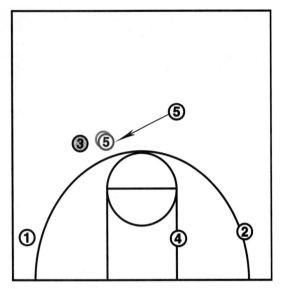

Diagram 6.30 Use Trail Screen

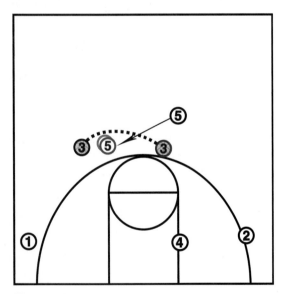

Diagram 6.31

KARL BROWN

I must also mention a foreign junior college point guard we came across. My assistant, Kevin Cantwell, took me to Chipola Junior College in Florida to watch Karl Brown from Leicester, England. At first I was not impressed. Karl was not super quick and was a below-average shooter and a fair passer. I then noticed how he defended on the ball. He constantly moved his feet and was always hounding the dribbler.

Normally, after recruiting a player, the first thing you have to teach him is defense. Karl was the reverse. His forte as a point guard was defense on the ball. He told me his fast feet came from playing soccer in England. I told him I didn't know anything about soccer but we would offer him a scholarship, which he gladly accepted.

In his first year at GT, I came close to telling Karl to hit the road, but he hung on, and when we recruited Kenny Anderson the next year, Karl's role and attitude took a tremendous turn. Karl came off the bench his senior year and completely turned games around with his defense on the ball. The ACC had some great point guards as always, and Karl would love to hound them and wear them down. Then a fresh Kenny Anderson would come back in and be impossible to guard. I kept Karl in the game for a while when Kenny came back and let them play together. It relieved Kenny defensively and, of course, Kenny could score, so Karl got him the ball.

One of the most memorable games I ever coached in was against LSU in the second round of the 1990 NCAA Tournament in Knoxville, Tennessee. Dale Brown had given me one of my all-time worst losses in Atlanta in the 1986 Final Eight game with Mark Price and John Salley. I wanted revenge, but the Shaquille O'Neal and Stanley Roberts inside combo was very, very intimidating. They also had a pretty good point guard in Chris Jackson. We went down 19 early and things looked very bleak. I sent Karl Brown in and he immediately guarded Chris Jackson all out, full court. Karl's defense instantly changed the game and lifted our team's spirits. We regained our confidence and came back for a great GT victory. Two more wins would take us to the Final Four, but this was our defining moment, and we owe it to Karl's defense. When you're watching point guards, study their feet and maybe you can find a Karl Brown for your team. Karl averaged an incredible 27 minutes for our 1990 Final Four team. After a very successful pro career in England, Karl is currently coaching there.

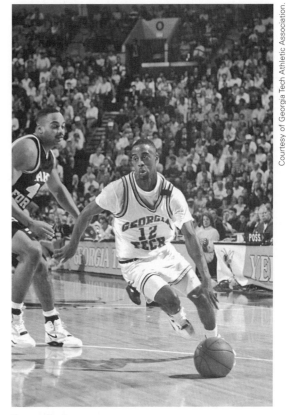

Kenny Anderson

KENNY ANDERSON

By now we had recruited some nationally ranked high school players, including Bruce Dalrymple, a New York slashing guard, to go along with Mark Price and Dennis Scott, who was National High School Player of the Year.

During the summer I would always go to New York to lecture at Jack Curran's basket-ball camp. Coach Curran is the legendary coach at Archbishop Molloy High School in Queens, New York. I played against Molloy and Coach Curran when I was at All Hallows High School in the Bronx. Coach Curran also played at All Hallows, but more important, he played at St. John's University for my college coach, Hall of Famer Frank McGuire.

Coach Curran had the utmost respect for Coach McGuire, so when I was an assistant for Coach McGuire it was very easy for me to have access to Coach Curran's practices. Another New York scout named Harry Gotkin also loved Coach McGuire, so every time I would go to New York to recruit, I would start at Molloy High School with Coach Curran and Harry Gotkin. Besides basketball, Coach Curran is also a legendary baseball coach and one of the most dedicated people I have ever met. At age 77 he's still going strong at Molloy.

While at his camp this particular summer, Coach Curran told me a freshman would be starting for him next season. At this point I knew Coach Curran well enough to know that he never started freshmen on his varsity team. I told the Coach Curran that I had to meet this freshman, so he called Kenny Anderson over and introduced us. I then watched Kenny play and he immediately reminded me of one of my all-time favorite players, Bob Cousy of the Boston Celtics. Like Bob Cousy, Kenny was a magician with the ball. He could put it between his legs and behind his back without hesitation. Also like Cousy, he could really see the courts and make passes you just don't ordinarily see. Kenny could also score at will. His shot wasn't pure, but he could make it a lot and especially when he needed to. He was very skinny, but his incredible skills made his strength irrelevant.

Also like Cousy, Kenny would put on a show in the open court. He was very mature for his age and some people wondered how much better he could get. At times he was so good it was nerve-wracking recruiting him. When you're recruiting possibly the best point guard ever to come out of New York, you can't miss a beat. His late mom, Joan, and I got along very well. My assistant Kevin Cantwell and I got to know

the staff at the Marriott LaGuardia Airport hotel very well while recruiting Kenny.

Mark Price was becoming an NBA star and that showed Kenny we would allow him to play his game. I told Kenny a lot about Dennis Scott and Brian Oliver. He liked very much that we had a great shooter he could set up and a slasher like Brian who could finish going to the basket. That trio would eventually become Lethal Weapon III, but Kenny could see beforehand how these two players could help his game evolve.

I'll always remember when he called and told me he was coming to Georgia Tech. We instantly became "Point Guard University." I also remember his first week on campus. His recruiting was so publicized I thought the rest of the team would resent this star treatment. I quickly realized how wrong I was.

NCAA rules prohibited us from watching our players play, so I anxiously awaited word from the other players. Brian and Dennis and everyone else loved playing with Kenny because he got them the ball at the right time and place. They told me he wouldn't shoot. So I called Kenny in and asked, "What's up with the non-shooting?" He told me not to worry, that he wanted to make sure he got off on the right foot with his teammates and wanted to gain their confidence. That's how smart a player he was.

I only got to coach Kenny for two years. As National Freshman of the Year, he led us to an ACC championship and the NCAA Final Four. I still feel today had he not gotten in foul trouble against UNLV we would have won a national championship. He's still upset at me for taking him out. He tells me he could have played with four fouls. He might have been right.

He once scored 50 points against Loyola Marymount, but his best game was when he had 4 points and 18 assists against nationally ranked UNC. Unfortunately for Kenny and us, we lost junior Dennis Scott to the NBA after that UNLV game. With Brian being a senior, Kenny suddenly lost two key parts to his overall game. It was impossible to replace Brian and Dennis, so Kenny was very frustrated at times during his sophomore year. He tried to do too much at times to help us win, and this took away from his great passing ability.

He was a consensus first-team all-American in 1991 and made second team in 1990. His freshman year he set a Georgia Tech season record for assist average (7.0) and also averaged 20.6 points per game. He was drafted second overall by the New Jersey Nets. He was an NBA All-Star his second year, but then after being traded three times he never really settled in to have the NBA career I am sure he had envisioned.

Ironically, late in his career he played for Boston. He was playing great, and seeing him on that famous parquet floor where Bob Cousy did his thing was fun to watch. However, once again he was traded and he was really despondent to have to leave the Celtics. He's doing better now and is beginning to coach in the development league. There's no doubt he could be a great teacher of the point guard position.

The key with Kenny was simple: get the ball in his hands. Once you did that, he took

care of everything else. Defenses tried to deny him passes, so we were constantly screening for him so he could receive a pass (Diagrams 6.32 and 6.33).

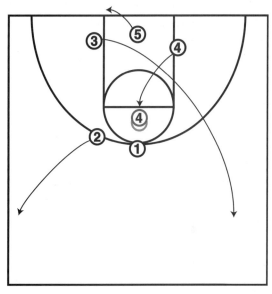

Diagram 6.32

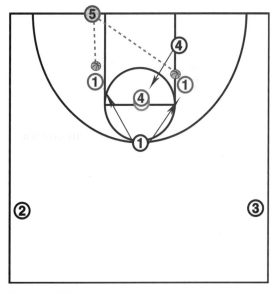

Diagram 6.33

TRAVIS BEST

After losing Dennis Scott early, we were prepared to lose Kenny after his sophomore season. We recruited two very good point guards to replace Kenny. We now could get involved with the top national point guards, and that's exactly what we did in recruiting Cory Alexander out of Virginia and Travis Best out of Springfield, Massachusetts. Cory planned on signing early and Travis late, so we concentrated more on Cory.

I loved Cory's size and how he could attack the rim. I didn't expect to see another Kenny Anderson for a while, so I definitely felt Cory with his versatility was as good a point guard as we could find. Cory loved our previous point guards' success, so it looked like a lock for us. On my last home visit to Cory, he surprised me and my assistant, Sherman Dillard, by informing us that he had changed his mind and decided to sign late. Since I already knew Travis was signing late, when Cory asked if I would wait for him I said sure. Upon leaving Cory's house, Sherman apologized for not being aware of Cory's change of mind. He also said we were behind with Travis and needed to make up some ground quickly.

Sherman went to see Travis the next day while I had to get back to campus for a previous commitment. Sherman called and, after making sure I was sitting down, informed me that Travis also had a change of mind and wanted to sign early with us. I now had to inform Cory of Travis's new game plan, and Cory was very upset with me.

Travis Best

I tried to explain to Cory that I couldn't turn Travis down. He was, like Cory, an outstanding prospect. Travis at 5 feet 11 inches was a great lefty shooter with range just short of Dennis Scott. He was built like a fullback and was explosive to the hole. His strength made him an excellent defensive player. While not the passer Kenny was, he wasn't far off. Travis had scored 73 points in one of his high school games. He was a great kid, a gentleman, and a good student, and once again we felt very fortunate to have another special point guard.

Travis, like Mark Price, could score with the ball and off the ball and with his strength could also post up. We ran lots of similar plays that I previously showed for Travis.

We came close to getting to the Final Four with Travis. In 1992, after the miracle in Milwaukee where James Forrest's incredible 3-point shot beat USC and put us in the Sweet 16, we lost a tough overtime game to Memphis State and Penny Hardaway. Travis lived up to his billing. He led us to an ACC championship in 1993 and was second-team all-American in 1995. He was a great scorer for us: sixth all-time at Georgia Tech, third in 3-point field goals, second in career assists, and 14th in ACC career assists.

He was a first-round pick of Indiana and was doing great there before being traded. He's currently playing overseas. His dad, Leo, was a heck of a player and Leo was very proud of Travis. With Mark Price, Craig Neal, Kenny Anderson, and Travis Best we were on a roll, and it was lots of fun for everyone.

Courtesy of Georgia Tech Athletic Association.

Jon Barry

THE BARRY BROTHERS

Every Final Four is in conjunction with the National Association of Basketball Coaches annual meeting, and it was there that I ran into Rick Barry. Rick, one of the NBA all-time greats, was being honored as part of that year's silver anniversary team. I had met Rick before and he started telling me about one of his sons, Jon, who was finishing his junior college career at Paris Junior College in Texas.

We had just lost our top wing recruit to UNC, so I was all ears. Rick sold me so much that I got Jon's number and left the dinner to call him. I told Jon I was so impressed with what Rick had said that I was offering him a scholarship and I was really hoping he would accept because I was very tired and wanted to get recruiting over with. Jon said he was sure he would accept, but asked if I minded if he made an official visit so he could see the school. I sent my assistant, Kevin Cantwell, out to see Jon and he told me Jon played all out. Thus began our relationship with the Barry family. The eldest, Scooter, played at Kansas for Larry Brown; Brent, now an NBA star, was a freshman at Oregon State; and the youngest, Drew, who we would later recruit, was in high school.

Jon was what we call a "sleeper" in the recruiting world. He was good enough to play anywhere in the country. He simply was a late developer. I don't believe I ever coached a better passing scoring guard than Jon. Like Craig Neal, he needed to be toned down at times, but his all-out play made him special. Jon had to replace Brian Oliver and Dennis Scott and gain Kenny Anderson's confidence. He just about did it when nobody believed he had a chance. His second and senior year with us he played alongside Travis Best and wouldn't leave the locker room after that tough loss to Memphis State. Recruiting the right junior college player at the right time can turn your program around or keep it going at a high level. Jon did that for us.

We loved having Jon come off staggered screens. If the shot was there, he took it; if it wasn't, he put it on the floor and became a point guard (Diagrams 6.34–6.36).

Over only two seasons at Tech, he averaged 16 points per game, shot 37 percent from the 3-point line, averaged 5 assists, and in his senior year led us in assists. He was a first-round pick in 1992 and, after playing 16 years in the NBA, now serves as an NBA TV analyst for ESPN.

Jon had told us about the youngest Barry, his brother Drew. The boys had a new stepdad,

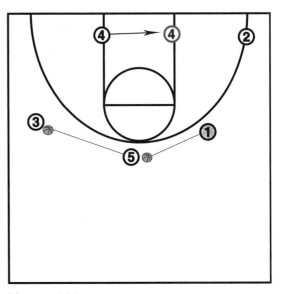

Diagram 6.34

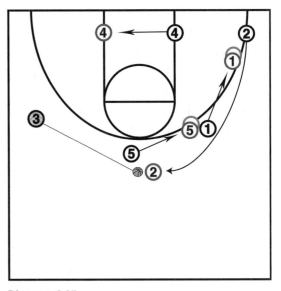

Diagram 6.35

Willie Connolly, whom they all liked very much. So off went my assistant Kevin Cantwell to San Francisco to evaluate Drew. Kevin thought Drew needed a red-shirt year but was very smart and had those Barry genes. Drew

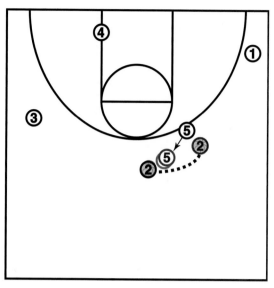

Diagram 6.36

Drew Barry

was more of a true point guard who played at a slower pace and was very cerebral. He definitely lacked strength, but his knowledge of how to play and find the open man forced us to insert him in the starting lineup very early in his career. As a freshman playing with Travis Best, he helped us win the 1993 ACC Tournament. In 1996, playing with Stephon Marbury, he led us to a regular-season championship and Sweet 16 appearance.

Drew is the GT career record holder for assists (724) and ranks 11th in ACC history. While leading us in assists, he also averaged 10.5 points per game, 13.3 over his last two seasons. He was Academic All-ACC and drafted by Seattle in 1996 in the second round. I highly recommend recruiting players who have a special feel for the game. They may lack certain skills or, as in Drew's case, strength, but there's no substitute for intelligence.

Drew's ability to inbound the ball in late-game situations won us a lot of games. I love smart inbounders. Drew also knew how to get our best player the ball when we needed a basket. Because of his strength, his defense was limited, but his brilliant positioning allowed him to take lots of charges. He may be the smartest player I ever coached. I wanted to hire Drew at College of Charleston; however, he's a successful businessman in Atlanta. There's no doubt in my mind he would be a very successful coach. The Barry boys were a joy to coach and I am very grateful I ran into Rick at that Final Four dinner.

STEPHON MARBURY

I felt we could never recruit a more highly publicized player than Kenny Anderson; however, New York once again was producing a very special point guard. Stephon Marbury was a public school product out of Lincoln High School in Brooklyn. We had two important factors in our favor regarding Stephon's recruiting. One, he loved Kenny Anderson and, two, he knew our starting point guard, Travis Best, was a senior and he could step right in. I remember flying to New York to watch Stephon play. I kept saying to myself that he couldn't be as good as Kenny. It took only a few minutes to realize that, although he was different than Kenny, he was indeed a special player.

Stephon was like a man playing with boys. He was strong like Travis Best and drove to the basket like nobody I've ever seen. He was fearless and had great range, but constantly attacked the rim and scored at will.

Courtesy of Georgia Tech Athletic Association.

Stephon Marbury

It was easy to see he was a scoring point guard and not a pure point guard, but with his talent I thought he could do whatever he needed to do. I watched his desire to win and I felt with this desire he would do whatever was needed to help his team win.

His high school coach, Bobby Hartstein, got sick and had to go to the hospital on our first official meeting with Stephon and his family. I was lost when I got to Stephon's building, so this little kid asked me if I was looking for Stephon. When I answered yes, he showed me the way. He told me he was Stephon's cousin and his name was Sebastian Telfair. Years later when I was out of coaching and in TV I did the Nike Hoop Summit in Memphis and watched Sebastian play. I kept saying to myself that I could have been back in Stephon's building recruiting another special point guard. Only in New York.

Stephon's family was like the Barry family. Stephon had older brothers, one who had been a star at the University of Georgia. He also had a younger brother, Zach, who would eventually play at Rhode Island. We talked a lot about Kenny Anderson and, of course, the fact that we were losing our star point guard, Travis Best. We had a great immediate playing opportunity. My assistant, Kevin Cantwell, once again did a great job, and we once again signed the best point guard in the country.

Unlike Kenny, Stephon's beginning was very different. I knew he couldn't see the court like Kenny. He was trying to do too much and not setting his teammates up like Kenny did with Dennis Scott and Brian Oliver. We got off to a horrible start and got upset by Santa Clara University (yes, Steve Nash was in that game), Bradley University, and Mount St.

Mary's University. We were in serious trouble heading into the ACC. Stephon, to his credit, realized this and we decided to change his game for the betterment of the team. He now concentrated on setting up his teammates while continuing to attack the rim. His new attitude completely turned us around. We went on to win 13 ACC games and an ACC regular-season championship. I still wanted Stephon to score and at times when we needed a bucket he would do his thing, but he showed me he was a winner and would do what was necessary for his team to win.

His strength made him an excellent defender and rebounder. In 1996, we lost to Wake Forest in the ACC tournament final when Tim Duncan forced Stephon to take a tough late-game shot when we were down 1. We played brilliantly versus Austin Peay State University and Boston College to get to the Sweet 16. However, Bob Huggins's Final Four University of Cincinnati team shut us down in Lexington in the third round. Stephon averaged 18.9 points as a freshman but was second to Drew Barry in assists (4.5). He was named ACC Rookie of the Year, first-team All-ACC, freshman all-American, and third-team all-American.

Stephon was so athletic that we put in some lobs and isolation plays for him (see Diagrams 6.37–6.42).

Lob Plays

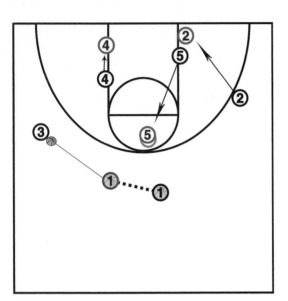

Diagram 6.37 Stephon's Lob

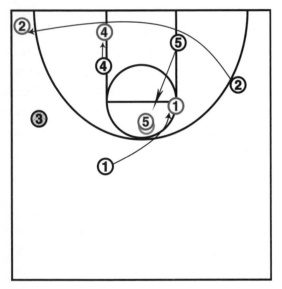

Diagram 6.38

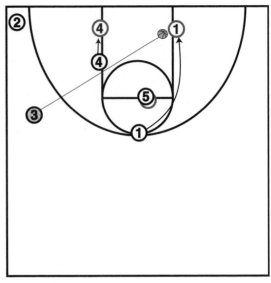

Diagram 6.39

Stephon left after his freshman season and was selected number four in the NBA draft. I loved it when he was in Minnesota with Kevin Garnett. That duo broke up, and Stephon went on to New Jersey, Phoenix (for Jason Kidd), and later to the New York Knicks. The Knicks do their preseason camp at the College of Charleston, and Stephon bought us a beautiful television for our locker room. He gets criticized for not being on a championship team and I know this frustrates him.

He came through for us and I am pulling hard for him. Stephon did the right thing leaving early for the NBA. He had every right to pursue financial security for himself and his family. The mistake I made was lacking foresight and not recruiting right behind Stephon. I thought Stephon might stay two years. I never had a player leave after one year

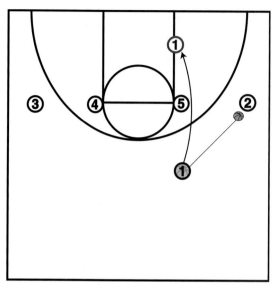

Diagram 6.40 Stephon Isolation

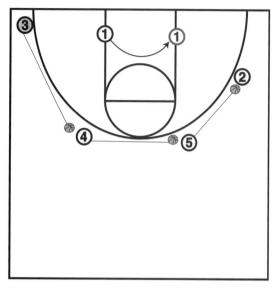

Diagram 6.42

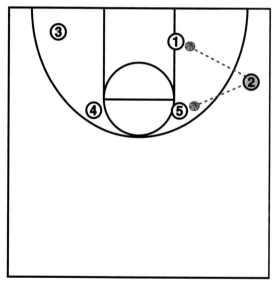

Diagram 6.41

and freshmen didn't leave back then the way they do today.

I've seen a lot of coaches make the mistake I did. We lost a great coach and person in Wake Forest coach, Skip Prosser, who passed away in July 2007. I remember doing a Wake Forest game on TV. I watched Chris Paul practice and play, and I told Skip that Chris would never stay four years and he better be preparing for Chris to leave at any time. Skip assured me Chris was different and wouldn't leave too soon. However, Chris couldn't turn down being a top-10 pick and did leave. Skip was surprised and got caught without a point guard. The result was Wake going from first to last. Chris spoke and cried at Skip's funeral, and it was easy to see what a wonderful relationship they had.

Coaches have to assume any outstanding player could leave at any time and they must somehow protect their team and program from falling too hard. By lacking foresight we put ourselves and our new recruits in a tough situation. It was very unfair to, all of a sudden, recruit players late and expect them to fill Stephon's or our previous point guards' shoes. After two years of struggling, we finally felt we had a point guard who could get us back. Tony Akins was a local player, originally from Michigan. He was another lefty, was quick, and could score and pass. He did lack strength but definitely had the skills. Tony played very well at times early on, but we couldn't get the right support around him. Dion Glover, a superb wing, unfortunately tore his ACL the first day of practice his sophomore year and turned pro that same year. Yes, I again lacked foresight on Dion.

Al Harrington, a great high school player out of Trenton, New Jersey, and our number one recruit, looked like he was coming but at the end decided to skip college and enter the NBA draft. That really caught me off guard. Al's a great kid and I had envisioned Dion and Al supporting Tony on the wings. I only coached Tony for two years, but I was very happy to see him play well for my successor, Paul Hewitt. A dark cloud was looming over our program, and Paul came in and removed that cloud and brought back the excitement and enthusiasm our program once had.

FROM GEORGIA TECH TO THE COLLEGE OF CHARLESTON

I expected to sit out one or two years and get back in the game. It turned out to be six years and, just when I thought I would never coach again, the College of Charleston job opened up in June 2006.

Greg Marshall, the outstanding young coach at Winthrop had accepted the job but after two days went back to Winthrop. Greg is now at Wichita State but there is unbelievable irony in my getting back into coaching by someone pulling a "Bobby Cremins."

I had covered some of their games for TV and I knew they had a pretty good senior guard by the name of Dontaye Draper coming back. Dontaye was a combo guard but had some special skills. Big schools had passed him over because of his size (5 feet 10 inches). I was definitely ready to get back in, but with a senior guard like Dontaye I thought we could have a built-in special guard. I was right.

Dontaye was great off the dribble, had range, toughness, and experience, and could really pass the ball. I wasn't sure if he could run a team. I felt this could make or break my first year back in coaching. Through the help of Dontaye's teammates, I learned that we could be a one-man team or that one man could get everyone else involved.

Dontaye got confused at first and at times didn't know when to shoot or pass. We were 3 and 6 and very much in danger of having a terrible year. Dontaye also had character. He hung in there with me and all of a sudden he busted out. He started to see the whole court, trusted his teammates, and scored when we most needed him. He started to put on a show and played as well as any point guard I have ever coached. From 3 and 6, Dontaye hit a game winner for a big conference win. We then won 19 of our next 23 games. Being down at halftime in the Southern Conference tournament opener, Dontaye led us back. In the semifinal game against a very good Appalachian State team, Dontaye scored 38 points and had 4 assists in a dramatic overtime win. We lost in the finals to Davidson, but Dontaye Draper left everything on the court.

The previous staff had run some special plays for Dontaye that I decided to keep, and I also added some old Georgia Tech plays that I already showed you.

- Dontaye passes to 2 and runs a UCLA cutoff 5 (Diagram 6.43).
- 5 then turns toward 1 and 1 will slice back off 5 (Diagram 6.44).

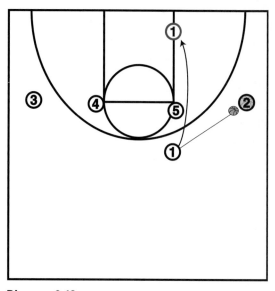

Diagram 6.43

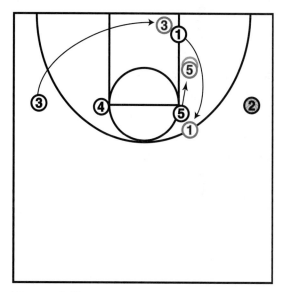

Diagram 6.44

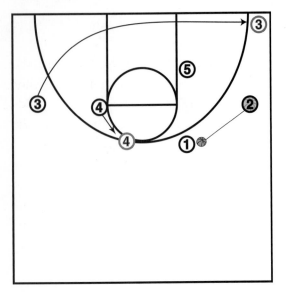

Diagram 6.45

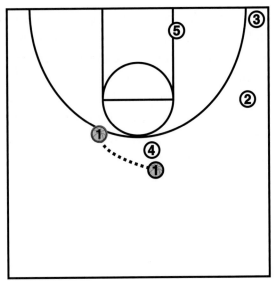

Diagram 6.47

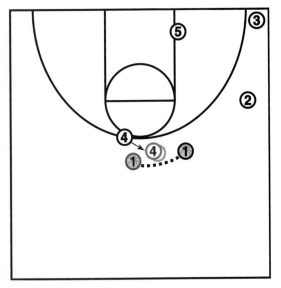

Diagram 6.46

- 2 passes to 1, 4 steps up to screen for 1 (Diagram 6.45).
- 4 screens for 1 who has a whole side to make a play. 4 will spot up (Diagrams 6.46 and 6.47).

The play can be run on either side.

Dontaye is presently playing in Australia's Top Division. I feel he can play in the NBA. He really made my first year back a very enjoyable one.

Dontaye's successor is Tony White Jr., who I recruited in July 2006 when I was hired. Tony was headed to prep school, but I convinced him to come to Charleston where I could red-shirt him his freshman year. However, he played very well in preseason and won the backup job to Dontaye and played 20 minutes for our 22-11, 2006–07 team. Tony's dad was an all-American shooting guard at Tennessee. Tony can shoot and is very quick but only weighed in at 140 pounds his freshman year.

He's a skinny combo guard, but I believe he will become special by his junior or senior year. He has a great attitude and will be spending a lot of time in the weight room during the off-season.

We also signed 6-foot freshman, Quasim Pugh, from Brooklyn, New York, who had a lot of natural point guard tendencies. As you can see, our point guard play can really make our offense free flowing and that's exactly what we want.

Afterword

I first started this guide to the ultimate offense three years ago while working as a TV analyst. Then my life completely turned around when I returned to coaching. This book had to be put on the back burner as I undertook the challenge of building another basketball program.

Although my new coaching job delayed the completion of this book, it has more importantly made this book more informative and much more interesting.

I have always loved fast-break basketball. I grew up playing point guard and watching Bob Cousy. I wanted to be an NBA player like Cousy, but failing in that quest led me to my true destiny of coaching. I had the pleasure to spend some time with Bob a few years ago at a charity golf event, and he told me that, as a coach, he absolutely loved teaching fast-break basketball because so many great and exciting plays happen in the open court. I agree.

As a coach, I also know the importance of a great secondary attacking pressure since so many coaches love pressure defense. I feel you must be able to run some half-court sets both man and zone. I continue to try and find more time in practice to work on special situations. What a feeling to work on a last shot and then see your team execute that play and win the game.

I hope you enjoyed the point guard stories in this book, but I've been very fortunate to coach a lot of great players who were not point guards. I hate to leave some of them out, but hopefully there will be another book where I can talk about them. Every great point guard needs those wings and posts to make it all happen.

Writing this book has made me a better coach. Yes, it has made me reflect on all those great games in my past, but just as important it has motivated me to have those moments again. In the two years since I started coaching again, I have already experienced some of those moments and hopefully more are to come.

When I was a young coach, I loved picking up a book and finding new ideas that made me a better coach. I hope this book will do that for you. Please e-mail any questions or comments to me at creminsb@cofc.edu.

Index

About the Author

Born July 4, 1947, Bobby Cremins, a native of Bronx, New York, graduated from the University of South Carolina in 1970 with a B.S. in business administration. He received an M.S. degree in guidance and counseling in 1977, also from University of South Carolina. A three-year starting point guard for the University of South Carolina under legendary head coach Frank McGuire, Cremins led the Gamecocks to some of their most successful seasons, including a 25–3 record (14–0 in the Atlantic Coast Conference) his senior year. Cremins played one year of professional basketball in Ecuador and was a 1972 selected Olympic tryee. He began his coaching career at Point Park College in Pittsburgh in 1971. He returned to his alma mater as an assistant coach to McGuire in 1972.

After a two-year stint at USC, Cremins was chosen to build the Appalachian State program, becoming the youngest Division I head coach at age 27. After a first-year mark of 13–14, the Mountaineers posted a five-year record of 87–56 while capturing three Southern Conference titles. His 1978–79 Southern Conference championship team earned an NCAA bid with a 23–6 record.

In 1981, Cremins took over a Georgia Tech program that had gone 4–23 the year before. Just four seasons later, Cremins and the Yellow Jackets claimed the first of their three ACC tournament titles. Cremins guided Tech to 14 winning seasons and 14 postseason berths in his 19 years and a Final Four appearance in 1990. He earned three ACC Coach of the Year awards (1983, 1985, 1996) while twice being named National Coach of the Year (1985, 1990).

Cremins thrust Georgia Tech into the national picture with a long line of great players, beginning with Mark Price and John Salley, and continuing with Craig Neal, Duane Ferrell, Tom Hammonds, Dennis Scott, Brian Oliver, Kenny Anderson, Jon Barry, Travis Best, Drew Barry, Stephon Marbury, and Matt Harpring. Under Cremins, Tech had 6 all-Americans, 23 all-ACC players, and 8 ACC "Rookie of the Year" honorees.

In the summer of 1986, Cremins was an assistant coach under Lute Olson for the U.S. team that won the World Championship in Spain. Two years later, Cremins was the head coach for the U.S. team's qualifying games in Mexico City. In the summer of 1996, Cremins added to his already impressive coaching résumé by serving as an assistant coach to Lenny Wilkens for the 1996 U.S. Olympic basketball team that earned a gold medal in Atlanta at the Centennial Olympic Games.

While out of coaching, Cremins worked for FOX Sports Net and Jefferson-Pilot Raycom doing color commentary and local TV shows. He also spent time doing motivational speaking, basketball clinics, basketball camps, and charity golf outings, including Coaches vs. Cancer and the Jimmy V.

In July 2006 he became the coach at the College of Charleston where he is currently in his third season.

Cremins and his wife, Carolyn, have three children: Liz, Suzie, and Bobby III.